Management Extra

QUALITY AND OPERATIONS MANAGEMENT

Management Extra

QUALITY AND OPERATIONS MANAGEMENT

Routledge
Taylor & Francis Group

LONDON AND NEW YORK

eLEARN

First published 2005 by Pergammon Flexible Learning
Revised edition 2008 by Pergammon Flexible Learning

Published 2013 by Routledge
2 Park Square, Milton Park, Abingdon, Oxfordshire OX14 4RN
711 Third Avenue, New York, NY 10017, USA

First issued in hardback 2016

Routledge is an imprint of the Taylor & Francis Group, an informa business

Notice
No responsibility is assumed by the publisher for any injury and/or damage
to persons or property as a matter of products liability, negligence or
otherwise, or from any use or operation of any methods, products,
instructions or ideas contained in the material herein.

British Library Cataloguing in Publication Data
A catalogue record for this book is available from the British Library

Library of Congress Cataloging-in-Publication Data
A catalog record for this book is available from the Library of Congress

ISBN 13: 978-1-138-14790-4 (hbk)
ISBN 13: 978-0-08-055236-1 (pbk)

Contents

List of activities   vii

List of figures   viii

List of tables   ix

Introduction: managing quality operations   xi

1 The language of quality   **1**

What is quality?   1

What is TQM?   8

Recap   18

More @   18

2 Improvement   **20**

You and your customers   20

Approaches to improvement   26

Improvement tools and techniques   31

Employee involvement   37

Recap   43

More@   43

3 Operations management   **45**

Quality in operations   45

Better by design   SO

Operations planning and control   57

Quality control tools and techniques   63

Recap   71

More @   72

4 Techniques for planning and control   73

Capacity planning and control   73

Inventory planning and control   78

Supply chain management   87

Recap   92

More @   93

5 Quality in health, safety and environment   **94**

Health, safety and the environment   94

Recap   102

More@   102

References   **103**

Activities

Activity 1	The quality issue	4
Activity 2	Quality management in your organisation	13
Activity 3	TQM	16
Activity 4	You and your customers	24
Activity 5	Kaizen	29
Activity 6	Improvement tools and techniques – cause and effect diagrams	36
Activity 7	You and your team	41
Activity 8	Quality in operations	48
Activity 9	Design in operations	55
Activity 10	Operations planning and control	61
Activity 11	Six sigma	67
Activity 12	Capacity planning and control	77
Activity 13	Inventory issues	83
Activity 14	The supply chain	90
Activity 15	Quality in health, safety and the environment	98

Figures

1.1 The stages of TQM   12
1.2 The EFQM excellence model   15
2.1 The organisation as a transformation process   21
2.2 The PDCA cycle   28
2.3 Flow chart for customer query at Kaston Pyral Services   32
2.4 Scatter diagrams at Kaston Pyral Services   33
2.5 Pareto diagram at Kaston Pyral Services   34
2.6 The basic structure of a cause and effect diagram   35
2.7 Cause and effect diagram at Hewlett-Packard   35
3.1 The organisation as a transformation process: operations   45
3.2 Management operations and support functions   47
3.3 Systems diagram of the provision of a guard   56
3.4 Push and pull control   58
3.5 Chart showing trends in variables or attributes   67
3.6 Control limits   67
3.7 Graph showing normal distribution   68
4.1 JIT uncovers problems   82
4.2 Materials requirements planning (MRP I) schematic   82
4.3 ERP   83
4.4 The organisation as a supply chain   87

Tables

1.1	The gurus of TQM	11
1.2	Pros and cons of TQM	16
2.1	NASA: Definition of customers	21
3.1	Different types of operations processes	46
3.2	Performance objectives and measures	59

Managing quality operations

Quality is a crucial concept for organisations. Attention to quality results in satisfied customers. It leads to new customers and to a more committed and confident workforce. It can improve products and services, cut down costs, boost productivity, keep inventory down, deliver customer satisfaction and positively affect both the top and the bottom line.

Operations management is equally important. Operations management is concerned with the way an organisation creates the goods and services on which it depends. For any organisation that is focused on delivering quality products and services to its customers, planning, controlling and continuously improving the quality of its operational processes has to be a core capability.

> **Good is not good where better is expected.**
>
> **Thomas Fuller (1608-1631) English clergyman and historian**

This book explores the associated concepts of quality and operations.

Your objectives are to:

♦ Develop your understanding of quality as an organisational, team and customer concept

♦ Explore and practice the application of quality tools and techniques to improve the quality of products, services and processes

♦ Evaluate how you can plan and control quality in the processes you manage

♦ Assess health, safety and the environment as quality issues.

1 The language of quality

Quality is not new. The Ancient Greeks used the word 'areté' meaning 'excellence' to define what they most admired physically and mentally in a man. Quality gradually became associated not just with human appearance and behaviour but also with the things they made. Craftsmen in the Renaissance used the word in their business to describe their highly finished and intricate jewellery, pottery, furniture silverware etc... Now the word seems to be applied to virtually everything. Footballers score quality goals, we give our children quality time, we complain about the quality of television and the weather, we talk about quality experiences. So what do we mean by quality?

In this theme, you will:

◆ Consider why quality concepts are important to organisational success

◆ Assess how total quality management extends thinking on quality management

◆ Explore two different standards for benchmarking of quality management systems.

What is quality?

The US army uses a strategic management approach called Total Army Quality (TAQ). This is aimed at the achievement of performance excellence through improvement, innovation, continuous learning and change.

Source: *US Army* (www)

As far as organisations and their products go, David Garvin (1984) has categorised five different definitions of quality based on the theories of quality gurus:

1 The **transcendent** approach – this is like areté, being synonymous with 'innate excellence', such as a quality player or quality diamond (24-carat). It's an absolute judgement.

2 The **manufacturing-based** approach – this is an approach associated with TQM guru Phillip B Crosby and is based on 'freedom from errors'. For example, a plastic cup may not have innate excellence like a handmade item of porcelain, but if it is manufactured according to its design specification, then it has quality. It is said to 'conform to requirements'.

3 The **user-based** approach – this interprets quality as 'fit for purpose', not only in terms of its specifications but also in terms of the specifications being appropriate from an end-user or customer point of view. For example, a plastic cup may have manufacturing-based quality, but it may not be appropriate for a garden party at Buckingham Palace. It not only lacks innate excellence, it is also not fit for the particular purpose of showing how refined people imbibe tea.

4 The **product-based** approach – this views quality as 'a measurable set of characteristics'. For example, so-and-so batteries are designed to last 120 hours, or 'this wood stain dries in 30 minutes'.

5 The **value-based** approach – this looks at quality in terms of cost and price. For example, flying easyJet is not everyone's idea of quality travel. On the other hand, it is good value as you can get from A to B at a much lower cost compared with a British Airways flight which also only gets you from A to B.

A customer approach to quality

It is normal to base any definition of quality around the customer, as in the user-based approach. Using this viewpoint is a key way of ensuring products conform to quality processes and requirements.

> **DeerQA: Focusing on Customers' Needs and Perceptions**
> Deer farmers understand that it's not what happens on the farm but what happens in the market – perhaps in a restaurant in New York or a delicatessen in Christchurch – that is the most important driving factor in their success. It's all about providing what the customers want. That's why the aim of the deer industry's quality programme is to provide its customers, worldwide, with an assurance that its products always meet their most discerning requirements.
>
> The DeerQA programme is always focused on consumers – their needs and their perceptions. At the same time, experience has shown that consistently meeting those needs also helps improve productivity (and therefore returns) on the farm. So it's a win/win result.

Source: *New Zealand Game Industry Board* (www)

Slack et al. (2001) use the following definition:

> Quality is consistent conformance to customers' expectations.

They use this definition because it seems to include all the best parts of the approaches mentioned previously. So, 'conformance' implies the specifications of the manufacturing-based approach; 'consistent' implies a controlled set of characteristics that can be measured as in the product-based approach; 'customers' expectations' implies a combination of the value and user-based approaches.

Although it is a useful definition, there are some drawbacks with it, as there are with others. For example, customers' expectations differ – some people liked the UK's Millennium Dome while others did not, but it was the same product for all. So who's to say what customers' expectations are? This is where marketing and market research comes in – to both create expectations and deliver to expectations. But then another point is that expectations and **perceptions** are not the same thing. What you might expect and what you perceive – i.e. your actual experience – of the product are two different things. So, from the organisation's point of view, it needs to ensure that the customers' perceptions of a product are that it meets their expectations. Customer feedback mechanisms come in handy for this.

> To summarise, quality from the organisational point of view involves a number of key dimensions:
>
> ♦ It is to do with excellence, however subjective.
>
> ♦ It is about setting specifications and standards – for example, in operations processes or product and service quality.
>
> ♦ Measurability is important – otherwise how do you know you have achieved quality? There is, therefore, the need for measurement tools.
>
> ♦ Value for money is relevant – prices and costs from both the customer and organisational point of view.
>
> ♦ It is about meeting customer needs or expectations.

These points will appear throughout this book.

Activity 1
The quality issue

Objective

In this activity, you will consider quality as an issue in your organisation. Use this activity to determine the application of the quality approach within your organisation and to assess its relevance.

Task

1 Complete the table by listing, as applicable, two to four examples of quality in your organisation for each of the five dimensions listed in the text. For example, find the use of the word excellence in company or personal documentation, such as in a mission or value statement, or list the quality standards and performance measures that you use. Find examples, probably in documentation, of the link between quality and cost/revenue issues. What examples are there in your organisation of customer-focused initiatives that you would say are quality based?

2 Discuss with your colleagues whether you have a quality approach in your organisation and assess its worth to the organisation and to yourselves, for example, does it work and add value to the organisation? Is your work of a better quality? Do you perform better as a team? Are there unacceptable 'costs' of quality? Should you adopt a quality approach (if you don't at present), and why?

Dimensions of quality	Applications in my organisation
Excellence	
Specifications and standards	
Measurability	
Value for money	
Customer focus	

Feedback

1   Your list could be something like this:

Dimensions of quality	Applications in my organisation
Excellence	It's mentioned in our mission statement We have an initiative called 'Towards manufacturing excellence' Commitment to excellence is one of my performance aims
Specifications and standards	We follow ISO 9000: 2000 All our products carry the CE marking We have our own quality assurance programme
Measurability	We use quality, cost, flexibility and reliability as performance objectives Departments use Pareto analysis Statistical process tools are used Level of customer complaints is one of our performance indicators
Value for money	'Added value' is mentioned in our supply chain management policy Departments use continuous improvement and six sigma statistical process control (SPC) to keep costs down
Customer focus	We have a dedicated call centre Internal servicing is based on service level agreements (SLAs) We have all been through a customer-care programme

2   A quality approach should lead to better organisational, team and individual performance as it involves excellence in what you do, which really should be the goal of everyone. However, some approaches can be over-formalised and consequently stretch people's patience and the organisation's wallet rather than stretching people's imagination and initiative. Focusing on 'process' rather than 'outcomes', as some standards do, is not a recipe for customer-focused excellence. It's important to define quality in a way that can be easily understood, implemented and measured by everyone concerned.

Products and services and quality

It is worth noting at this point that there is a difference between products and services and product and service quality.

Products are usually tangible entities such as chairs, cars, TVs and so on – 'goods' if you like. Services are intangibles such as staying in a hotel, going on a training course, dealing with your bank, getting your computer fixed.

Slack et al. (2001) suggest that the differences can be explained in several ways:

- **Tangibility** – you can physically touch products, but you cannot touch a consultancy service.

- **Storability** – products can be physically stored, but a service that provides accommodation for the weekend 'expires' once that weekend is over.

- **Simultaneity** – products are produced before the customer receives them, but services are usually produced at the same time as the customer receives them. For example, a CD is produced in a factory and moved to a retail outlet, but the service of selling the CD to the customer is simultaneous with its consumption.

- **Customer contact** – services generally involve a higher level of customer contact than products. How many customers get to see inside a factory?

As regards quality, Slack et al. (2001) note that product quality is simpler to judge as it is based on agreed physical standards, whereas service quality is more complex and subjective.

In service quality, we tend to judge not only the outcome of a service but also **the way it is produced** – something you wouldn't do if you were buying a computer. You wouldn't mind how it was produced as long as it conformed to the correct standards. But if you wanted a new pair of shoes and the assistant was rude, despite the fact that the service delivered the shoes you wanted, you would not be satisfied with the quality of the operation.

Many operations are in fact a mixture of products and services, and Slack et al. (2001) suggest that the distinction between them may not be particularly useful. For example, a restaurant provides food + food delivery + ambience, but as a customer you just buy one product – a meal for two at Il Forno.

Organisations increasingly refer to providing a 'product' even when they technically just provide a service. Having said that, it's important to note that there are some key differences, particularly in terms of judging quality.

Why is quality important?

The DeerQA programme case study highlights a key point about quality:

> ...experience has shown that consistently meeting those [customer] needs also helps improve productivity (and therefore returns) on the farm. So it's a win/win result.

Quality can improve productivity and the bottom line. In other words, quality not only keeps customers happy, it can improve productivity and profitability – reasons enough it seems for organisations to follow the quality route. But not the only reasons. Back to the New Zealand game industry again.

> The New Zealand Game Industry Board see the benefits of DeerQA on two levels – national and local. National in terms of tackling global concerns affecting the whole industry, and local in terms of individual farms, stock and station agents, transport operators and venison processing plants. This is summarised as follows.
>
> **DeerQA: Two complementary roles**
>
> | New Zealand | The farm |
> | --- | --- |
> | Quality Assurance | Quality Improvement |
> | *Market access* | *Reducing waste* |
> | animal welfare
animal health
environmental issues | bruising
hide damage |
> | *Food safety* | *Animal production* |
> | human health
residues | growth rates
fawning
reducing losses
velvet yields
genetic improvements
animal health |
> | *Animal welfare* | *Animal welfare* |
> | velveting
outdoor wintering
transport | velveting
'five freedoms' |
> | *Environment* | *Environment* |
> | sustainability | sustainability |

Source: *New Zealand Game Industry* (www)

This case study suggests that quality is important for both local and national reasons, such as environmental issues, animal welfare, food safety, waste reduction and market access.

It seems self-evident somehow that having a quality approach will lead to better market, business and financial performance as it includes giving customers what they want, cutting costs, utilising best practices in manufacturing goods and so on – a gold mine of good intentions. 'Consistent conformance to customers' expectations' also means:

- customers cost less to retain than to acquire
- the longer the relationship with the customer, the higher the profitability
- a loyal customer will commit more spend to its chosen supplier
- about half of new customers come through referrals from existing clients.

But it's important to bear in mind that there are costs to quality, and there can be a tailing off in performance over time. If implementation is poor and costs high, don't expect results overnight, if at all. The word 'continuous' is often used with quality to ward off any tailing off because if you drop your guard for a moment, someone else will overtake you, so quality has to be ongoing and improvement continuous. But how far can quality go?

What is TQM?

Total quality management (TQM) is arguably the most significant of the new ideas which have swept across the operations management scene over the last few years.

Source: *Slack et al.* (2001)

Total quality management is an extension of the concept of quality. Some might say *the* extension, as TQM takes the idea of quality in organisations to its *nth* degree.

There are as many definitions of TQM as there are definitions of quality, perhaps more. Here are a few of them.

TQM is...

An effective system for integrating the quality development, quality maintenance and quality improvement efforts of the various groups in an organisation so as to enable production and service at the most economical levels which allow for full customer satisfaction.

Source: *Feigenbaum* (1986)

Put simply, it involves everyone in an organisation and associated business processes co-operating to furnish products and services that meet their customers' needs and expectations.

Source: *Dale and Cooper* (1992)

...a transformation in the way an organisation manages. It involves focusing management's energies on the continuous improvement of all operations, functions, and above all, processes of work. Quality is really nothing more, therefore, than meeting customer needs. To do this, you must improve work processes, because it's the result of these processes that the customer cares about.

Source: *Cauldron* (www)

So, you might say TQM is all embracing as far as the organisation goes.

The key themes or concepts of TQM are as follows:

◆ Meeting the needs/expectations of internal and external customers – this is the goal of TQM, and it means looking at your business and its products/services from the customer's point of view. It means everyone is a customer, internally and externally. You are a consumer or customer of goods and services provided by other people/units in your organisation and you are a supplier of goods and services to other people and units in your organisation. Organisations use service level agreements (SLAs) to cement these internal relationships.

◆ Covering everyone in the organisation – everyone is involved, including the supply chain where appropriate (continuous improvement). Task and work group programmes such as job enrichment, job enlargement and job rotation may be used to enhance employee involvement and participation.

◆ Continuous improvement – TQM is not a one-off fix. It is ongoing and always looking for improvements. TQM is insatiable.

◆ Teamwork – a key theme in involving employees. 'People are our greatest asset' is a familiar slogan in TQM organisations.

◆ Top management commitment – a vital ingredient, and one of the common failings of TQM. TQM is a whole-organisation programme. It is strategic with long-term objectives. It frequently involves culture change. It must be led from the top otherwise the vision fades and it becomes diluted. Partial TQM is no good – it's all or nothing.

♦ Development of quality systems, standards, measures and tools – a systematic approach based on standards, performance measures and measurement tools is the nitty-gritty of TQM.

Check out some of the TQM buzzwords in the following example.

Quality Mission Statement
The Washington Cold Storage quality objective is to meet or exceed the expectations of our customers, both internal and external, through the continuous improvement of our systems and processes.

Quality Policy
Washington Cold Storage Inc. is committed to be a national best practice company within the competitive Food Storage Industry, attuned to understanding its markets and meeting or exceeding its customers' needs. It is our objective to adopt a Total Quality Management approach, integrating the principles of continuous improvement of our systems and processes, involving all our employees, and working in partnership with our customers and suppliers to ensure the storage of products meeting all regulatory requirements. Our commitment to quality extends to all functions and all levels of the organization. Through Total Quality Management the company will develop and maintain a culture which encourages and demands teamwork and participation in meeting our quality objectives. This policy assigns a responsibility for quality to all employees. The result will provide the basis for Washington Cold Storage to achieve competitive advantage and thereby prosper through growth and improved profitability. Washington Cold Storage Company is committed to the highest standards of personalized service and product management.

Source: *Washington Cold Storage Inc.* (www)

*You will learn more about the key ideas of TQM throughout **Quality and Operations***.

Before learning more about systems and standards in TQM, it will help your understanding if we go back a little and look at the development of TQM from both a theoretical and a practical standpoint.

The development of TQM

It is worth looking at TQM in two different ways – through the eyes of the theoreticians who developed it and as a natural extension of previous applications of quality management. Note that TQM developed as a manufacturing concept, but has now moved on to service organisations as well. This is why many of the processes have a manufacturing feel to them.

TQM: the gurus

TQM as a theory was developed after the Second World War by US academics such as Armand Feigenbaum and W. Edwards Deming. As a practical notion, it had its first major impact in Japan where American ideas caught on as part of the rebuilding of the country following the war. It then caught on in the West where it continues to be a source of fascination and debate. There is an important difference in timescale between East and West as regards quality and TQM. For example, the Deming Quality Award started in Japan in 1951, whereas the quality standard BS 5750 was not introduced in the West until 1979, and it wasn't until 1987 that the US introduced the Baldridge Award. Company-wide quality control was common in Japanese companies by the late 1970s, but did not begin in the West until the early 1980s. Table 1.1 outlines the contribution of some key thinkers on quality.

Gurus	Their contributions to TQM
A Feigenbaum	Responsible for the idea of total quality control which is popular in Japan – see *Total Quality Control* (1986)
W E Deming	Father of quality control. Emphasised quality as a top management and strategic activity. Famous for his '14 points for quality improvement' – see *Out of Crisis* (1986)
J M Juran	Emphasised a more user-based approach to quality management based on 'fitness for purpose'. Concerned with management responsibility for quality and the involvement of individual workers in quality improvements. See the Juran Institute website – www.juran.com
K Ishikawa	Originated quality circles and cause and effect diagrams. Saw quality circles as a way of involving employees to make TQM work
G Taguchi	Emphasised the importance of engineering in quality through design combined with statistical methods of process control. Originated the idea of quality loss on a product/service from the time it was created (quality loss function or QLF)
P B Crosby	The idea of cost of quality and zero defects was his main concern – he developed a zero defects programme in his book *Quality is Free* (1979)

Table 1.1 *The gurus of TQM*

Of course, many other gurus have also discussed the quality issue, the most notable books being Peters and Waterman (1982) *In Search of Excellence* and Peters and Austin (1984) *A Passion for Excellence*.

TQM: the stages

Another way of looking at TQM is the way it has developed as a concept of quality management. This is usually described in four stages:

1 **Inspection** – a basic, fire-fighting system of quality control involving error detection and correction.

2 **Quality control** – a more rigorous quality management system involving self-inspection, statistical process control (SPC) and quality standards.

3 **Quality assurance** – a preventative-based system emphasising product and process design, planning, and process control.

4 **Total quality management** – all the previous three and more – see Figure 1.1.

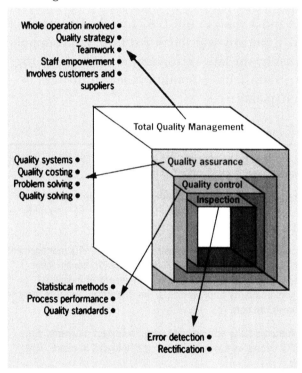

Figure 1.1 *The stages of TQM*   Source: *Slack et al.* (2001)

Each stage is a progression which absorbs the previous stage until you get to the final stage, which is TQM. The key development between total quality management and other forms of quality management is its strategic focus on empowerment and improvement. It involves maximising the potential of people right across the organisation in a continuing drive for improvement of all activities.

Activity 2
Quality management in your organisation

Objective

This activity asks you to assess the type of quality management your organisation has adopted.

Task

Where is your organisation on the quality journey?

Based on the development of quality through the four stages of quality management, explain how far your organisation has progressed and what processes it has adopted:

Stage of quality management	Tick	Comments
1 Inspection	☐	
2 Quality control	☐	
3 Quality assurance	☐	
4 TQM	☐	

Processes adopted to meet the stage of quality management in your organisation:

Feedback

Discuss your answer with your colleagues to see if they agree with your assessment.

Systems and standards

TQM is very concerned about quality systems and standards. A quality system is:

the organizational structure, responsibilities, procedures, processes and resources for implementing quality management.

Source: *International Organization for Standardization* (1994)

Quality standards are the guidelines or benchmarks which good quality systems adhere to or are compared against. Typically, quality systems and standards involve documentation – quality manuals, procedures manuals, work instructions and specifications and quality standards documents. In fact, this is one of the criticisms of TQM – there is too much documentation and systemisation and this stifles creativity.

The ISO 9000 series

Perhaps the most famous of the quality system standards is the quality management ISO 9000 series developed by the International Organization for Standardization (ISO), based in Geneva. ISO standards are an attempt to harmonise quality standards throughout the world.

The ISO 9000 series covers:

◆ quality management and quality assurance standards and guidelines for selection and use – ISO 9000

◆ a quality systems model for quality assurance in design/development, production, installation and servicing – ISO 9001

◆ a quality systems model for quality assurance in production and installation – ISO 9002

◆ a quality systems model for quality assurance in final inspection and test – ISO 9003

◆ quality management and quality system elements: guidelines – ISO 9004.

The ISO 9000 standards act as quality assurance to customers that products have been produced according to specific quality criteria. Hence, many organisations seek to gain a certificate proving they have quality management systems in place.

However, thinking of the ISO standards as order-winning criteria may be a mistake – there is an acknowledged danger that these standards can degenerate into just bureaucratic procedures. Accordingly, many organisations now view them as the beginning and not the end of quality management – they see them as order-qualifying. In other words, they are preliminary qualifications, whereas the goals of TQM, customer satisfaction, continuous improvement and so on, are the dynamic targets that organisations should be aiming for.

The EFQM excellence model

By way of comparison with ISO 9000, another set of standards for quality management is called the EFQM excellence model. It was devised by the European Foundation for Quality Management in 1988 and is based on quality in nine areas: leadership, policy and strategy, people, partners and resources, processes, customer results, people results, society results and key performance results – see Figure 1.2.

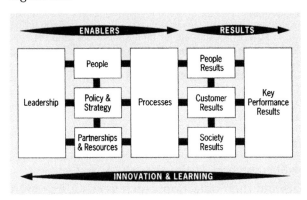

Figure 1.2 *The EFQM excellence model*Source: *European Foundation for Quality Management* (www)

The first five areas are enablers and the following four are concerned with results. The emphasis is on results, not just processes, and its use as a self-assessment tool differentiates it from the ISO 9000 series.

You may like to check out www.efqm.org for more information.

Pros and cons of TQM

> **I can only say that TQM sucks. It is a return to the stone age for the working person. It is nothing but stretch out and company unions wiping out worker gains and worker rights for the benefit of management. It is just another tool for manipulation. Nothing new about that.**

Source: *Posting on an Internet TQM discussion list*

There is an ongoing debate about the effectiveness of TQM. Table 1.2 summarises some of the salient points.

Arguments for TQM	Arguments against TQM
It can reduce product defect rates or customer complaints	Management is unable to make the necessary commitment
Getting employees on board improves productivity	Over-complex tools, systems and standards
People take pride in, and responsibility for, their products	It is stressful for employees who can be over-empowered
Quality cascades through the whole organisation at every level	The time and resources needed to implement it are too great
Quality throughout the supply chain improves product supply and distribution	It is impossible to improve continually
Continuous improvement keeps people challenged	People are expected to do more but are not paid any more
Everybody has a customer focus	TQM is not suitable for all organisations (and the culture change required is too great)
People use their brains to solve problems	It takes too long to implement
Reduces costs and improves bottom line	It increases costs and harms bottom line

Table 1.2 *Pros and cons of TQM*

Supporters of TQM will come back at the opposition and suggest that there are ways around their objections, such as ensuring reward systems that harmonise with any new tasks (taking a whole system view) or setting aside training days for management and staff. Whatever the opinions, TQM has thrown up a lot of ideas, and organisations do not have to implement it to benefit from some of these ideas, for example, some organisations implement teamworking practices even though they do not choose to adopt TQM.

Activity 3
TQM

Objective

Imagine your organisation wanted to adopt TQM. From a strategic point of view, what areas do you need to focus on? This activity asks you to develop a 10-point checklist for a TQM strategy.

Task

Draw up a 10-point checklist of the areas/activities a TQM programme should cover. For example, you could start with 'create a vision based on meeting customers' needs'.

1

2

3

4

5

6

7

8

9

10

Feedback

Here's our checklist. Yours should be similar. Check with your colleagues to see what they have written and discuss your answers.

1   Create a vision based on meeting customers' needs.

2   Secure top management commitment.

3   Devise quality systems and standards.

4   Develop a culture-change programme.

5   Develop a programme for continuous improvement.

6   Decide on which performance measures and quality-control tools to use.

7   Draw up a training and development plan to include managers.

8   Identify approaches to employee involvement, for example, teamworking, job redesign, quality circles.

9   Develop customer initiatives such as a customer-care programme.

10 Include health and safety and the environment in your approach.

◆ Recap

Consider why quality concepts are important to organisational success

- ◆ Quality means producing goods and services that continually meet the needs and expectations of the customer.

- ◆ Quality is important in attracting new customers, developing lasting relationships with existing ones, controlling costs and achieving a more committed workforce.

Assess how total quality management extends thinking on quality management

- ◆ TQM developed previous thinking on quality. It is a management philosophy concerned with improving all aspects of the operation's performance and, in particular, with the processes for managing improvement.

Explore two different standards for benchmarking of quality management systems

- ◆ A quality management system is the organisation's way of co-ordinating its activities to assure quality. It is the organisational structure, responsibilities, procedures, processes and resources for implementing quality management.

- ◆ Quality systems can be benchmarked against quality standards. ISO 9000 and the EFQM excellence model are two international standards for quality management.

▶▶ More @

Oakland, J. (2003) 3rd edition, *TQM: Text with Cases*, Butterworth-Heinemann
This book explores the evolution of TQM and how a TQM strategy can be applied to achieve world-class performance. It includes material on six sigma, the EFQM excellence model and ISO 9000:2000.

Porter, L. and Tanner, S. (2004) *Assessing Business Excellence*, Butterworth-Heinemann
This presents the key principles of business excellence and shows how you can actively drive improvement by reviewing your activities and results against holistic business excellence frameworks.

The **DTI** publishes an excellent, best practice toolkit aimed at helping you to manage implement, control and improve the quality of processes you manage. See www.dti.gov.uk/bestpractice/operations/quality.htm

The Institute of Quality Assurance website, www.iqa.org also offers a range of interesting publications and articles.

You can find more on the ISO 9000 series on the **International Organization for Standardization** website at www.iso.ch and on the EFQM Excellence Model at www.efqm.org which is the website for the **European Foundation for Quality Management**.

2 Improvement

Commitment to continuous improvement is a cornerstone of total quality management. Even the best organisation needs to improve to keep pace with the developing needs and expectations of its customers and with its competitors who will themselves be moving forward.

> **Quality is really nothing more, therefore, than meeting customer needs. To do this, you must improve work processes, because it's the result of these processes that the customer cares about.**
>
> Cauldron (www)

It follows then that the starting point for continuous improvement is to take stock of what it is that your customer needs and expects and to evaluate how well the quality of your product or service measures up.

In this theme, we look at how you can take a planned approach to continuous improvement and at how you can involve your team in making a similar commitment.

You will:

◆ Identify your customers and how to gain feedback on their needs and expectations

◆ Consider approaches to quality improvement and how you can apply them to the products or services you provide

◆ Explore a range of analytical tools and techniques for problem solving and quality improvement

◆ Consider how you can involve your team in improving quality and customer service.

You and your customers

Your customers

> We are a global, diverse family with a proud heritage passionately committed to providing outstanding products and services that improve people's lives.

Source: *Ford Motor Company* (www)

Before you can identify anybody's needs and satisfy expectations, you need first to find out who your customers are. The best way of looking at this is to think in terms of what you are supposed to be doing in your work area/organisation. If you view the organisation as a transformation process (see Figure 2.1), your purpose as part of this (your job role) is to convert inputs (what your suppliers bring in) to outputs. These outputs are what customers receive: products and services. This is also the starting point for operations management and the supply chain.

Figure 2.1 *The organisation as a transformation process*

If you ask yourself what your organisation outputs in terms of its products and services, there you will find your customers. Table 2.1 shows how the National Aeronautical and Space Administration (NASA) matches its customers to its products and services.

Agencywide	Service or Product	Description of Customers Served
Technical data and innovations	Tangible improvements in the quality of life	The American public and humanity
General information about space, aeronautics, and the planet Earth	Knowledge and inspiration Press releases and responses to the media Responses to requests from the public Publications NASA television programming	The American public, the media, and humanity
Cooperation in foreign policy initiatives	Contributions to national and international security and peace	The Administration, the Federal Government, and humanity
Educational programs	Programs and materials for K-12 Programs and materials for universities	Potential customers including all public and private primary and secondary schools, colleges and universities, as well as teachers, professors, and staff. Potential customers are all US students
High tech jobs and skills	Maintenance and improvement in US standard of living and technical capability	Industry, universities and the American public
Strategic Enterprise Units	**Service or Product**	**Description of Customers Served**
Aeronautics Enterprise	Access to Experimental Research Facilities Advanced computational methods	Aerospace and related companies, other Government
	Applied or validated technology Basic aeronautical technology	Agencies, and institutions of higher learning
	Technical expertise and assistance	Aerospace and related companies and other Government Agencies, universities, and approximately 300 other private sector companies
Space Technology Enterprise	New and innovative space technology to meet the challenges and lower the cost of future space missions Support for the expansion of commercial space industries Technology to revitalize access to space	Aerospace and non-aerospace companies, academia, other Government Agencies, and other NASA offices

Table 2.1 *NASA: Definition of customers*   Source: *NASA (www)*

NASA looks at customers from two perspectives. The first and broader Agencywide perspective is focused on our collective products of technical data and innovations; general information about space, aeronautics, and the planet Earth; cooperation in foreign policy initiatives; educational programs; and high-technology jobs and skills. The second perspective is focused on the services and products we specifically provide to our customers through the Strategic Enterprises.

Who are your suppliers?

If you have customers, you are a supplier, and your suppliers will view you as a customer. And that's not all, you have internal as well as external customers – don't forget them. The point is, when assessing customer needs, think about **everyone's** needs.

Also bear in mind that suppliers are increasingly important in quality management because they are a key link in the supply chain. For example, Nissan involves suppliers in new product development (NPD) improvements. Supplier involvement can greatly decrease time to market as well as reduce delivery costs. Without suppliers' input, how can you hope to deliver the quality service your customers expect?

What are your customers' needs/wants/ expectations?

This is something you should try to find out. Use questionnaires, interviews, surveys, feedback mechanisms and ask the right questions, like 'What do you think of the service you are getting?', 'How could it be improved?', 'What is most annoying about our service?' and so on.

The words 'needs', 'wants' and 'expectations' have become somewhat interchangeable in the customer context, although some would argue differently. Customer 'needs' are seen as basic requirements like empathy, reassurance and security, whereas customer 'wants' implies fulfilling all customer requirements. Expectations tend to be based on what the customer believes they should receive (customer satisfaction isn't enough) – 'achieving customer delight' or 'creating buyer excitement' are key slogans in this approach.

However you explain it, customers need/want/expect things like:

- ◆ value for money
- ◆ products/services that work
- ◆ delivery on time
- ◆ friendly service.

They need/want/expect quality.

How to satisfy (delight) customers

As you read the case study on Woburn Safari Park, think about the elements of its customer-care strategy, and the main benefits that resulted from its approach.

Winner: Woburn Safari Park

The winner of the Unisys/Management Today 2000 Service Excellence Award for Consumer Services was Woburn Safari Park.

When Chris Webster arrived in 1992, he found that staff regarded human visitors as 'public enemy number one'.

One culture/strategy change later, staff now engage the park's customers in conversation, they have been trained in customer care and they collect customer feedback and complaints.

There is an 'employee of the month' award and each employee is considered to be a 'walking information post', dealing with service failure on the spot. The products have been overhauled too, and a marketing programme put in place to boost visitor numbers.

By joining the Safari Club, customers can receive regular newsletters and invitations to special events, and there is a park website.

There is also special pricing for mothers with children after school and half-price tickets for locals.

Result – written complaints have halved, the employee headcount has doubled, visitor numbers have shot up and turnover has quadrupled.

Source: *adapted from Unisys/Management Today Service Excellence Awards* (2000)

Customer care

Customer care covers those initiatives the organisation takes to satisfy/delight its customers. Such initiatives usually have some or all of the following ingredients:

- using questionnaires/surveys/focus groups to identify customer needs
- making customer care part of employees' objectives
- setting standards for customer care
- training employees in customer care, such as telephone techniques
- speeding up delivery mechanisms
- setting up a customer service department

- developing product information
- improving communication channels
- rewarding employees for customer-care achievements
- improving the quality of goods sold and of the place where they are sold
- developing flexible pricing mechanisms
- catering for customers with special requirements, for example child friendly areas in shops etc.

Service level agreements

One way of improving customer care between customers and suppliers is known as the service level agreement or SLA. An SLA quantifies the minimum level of service quality a supplier will provide and a customer expects. They are frequently agreements between different departments **within** an organisation, or between partners of outsourcing organisations.

Typically, an SLA contains objectives and measurable targets, for example, 'answer the telephone within four rings'. It should also contain customer responsibilities, constraints and methods of delivery and monitoring.

The idea of SLAs is to establish trust between customers and suppliers and to diminish disruptions to the supply chain through lack of clear understanding of what is expected and what can be delivered. Critics argue that they may work against the very trust they are trying to establish through over-formalisation of the customer–supplier relationship.

Activity 4
You and your customers

Objective

Use this activity to identify who your customers and suppliers are and what they need from you.

Task

Use the opposite table to identify your customers and suppliers (both internal and external) and what services you should be providing for them.

Identify particular products/services, such as properly specified contracts, payment after 30 days, production reports every month, technical support, training activities, queries replied to within five days, etc.

Customers	What they need from me

Suppliers	What they need from me

Feedback

If you found this activity difficult to complete, you may need to do more work to find out what your customers need from you.

You could also discuss your answer with colleagues – and preferably with your customers and suppliers – to see if they agree with you.

Once you have gathered your lists together, look through them and identify how well you are meeting their needs. Think about and set priorities for some improvement areas.

Approaches to improvement

There are two main approaches to improvement in organisations:

◆ breakthrough improvement

◆ continuous improvement.

Breakthrough improvement

Breakthrough improvement, as the name implies, is a sudden change in the way an organisation operates. This may involve the introduction of new technology, moving to new premises, a change in culture or structure, or adopting a new system or process, such as implementing performance management, or a new type of reward system. Business process re-engineering (BPR) is a good example of the breakthrough improvement approach.

Joseph M Juran, one of the gurus of TQM, wrote a classic book, *Managerial Breakthrough* (1964), which was the first to describe a step-by-step sequence for breakthrough improvement, a process that became the basis for quality initiatives worldwide. Motorola pioneered a breakthrough approach in the 1980s based on Juran's work which became known as the Six Sigma Breakthrough. Check out the Juran Institute on www.juran.com for more information.

Continuous improvement

Kaizen means improvement. Moreover, it means improvement in personal life, home life, social life and work life. When applied in the work place, kaizen means continuing improvement involving everyone – managers and workers alike.

(1986)

A less radical approach than breakthrough improvement is an incremental, or gradual, approach called continuous improvement. This is also known as *kaizen* in Japan.

Have a look at the case study below, 'APW Mclean is Going Lean'. This shows continuous improvement using a systematic approach to identifying and eliminating waste called 'lean manufacturing', which contains many of the ingredients of TQM. Lean manufacturing is based on five principles:

- specify value in terms of the customer's needs
- identify the value stream for each product or service
- create continuous flow through the value stream
- produce goods or services according to the pull from the customer
- continue always to improve and seek perfection.

APW Mclean is Going Lean
APW Mclean Robbinsville, located in Mercer County, New Jersey, manufactures integrated thermal management products and is striving to improve its business operations to world-class competitiveness. Mclean builds products for the telecommunication, computer and data communication markets.

Their products include AC and DC motorized impellers, package blowers, fan assemblies, centrifugal blowers, and filter box fans for electronic systems. This 230-person company was founded in 1950, and has over 1,751,042,000 (1999) dollars in corporate (APW Applied Power) annual sales.

Greg Rees, Operations Leader of APW Mclean Robbinsville, was familiar with the Manufacturing Extension Program (MEP) through a previous work experience with Delaware Valley Industrial Resource Center (DVIRC), the MEP for the Philadelphia area manufacturers. DVIRC referred Mclean to New Jersey Manufacturing Extension Program Inc. (NJMEP).

Last September, NJMEP Field Agent, Jake Adams, and his counterpart from DVIRC, met with Mr. Rees and his staff. 'We discussed the company's need to reduce lead-time, improve on-time delivery performance and product quality,' explained Jake Adams.

One of Mclean's world-class strategies is to have all employees in the company participate in continuous improvement efforts. Through Mercer County Community College and DVIRC, Jake worked to implement the training exercises, which consisted of the Five Principles of Lean and the Eight Wastes in Manufacturing. The training integrated classroom lectures with a simulated factory to reinforce the employees' learning and retention. 163 employees participated in the training.

After the completion of the training, one department at a time will have a Kaizen blitz event (Kaizen means continuous improvement). The Kaizen event is when you take the Lean concept and apply it in the factory. Employees in the DC Motorized Impeller cell (DCMI) were the first group to apply the concepts they learned.

A positive impact has already been seen at Mclean, in the DCMI cell, by applying the Lean concept. The cycle time was reduced by 1400%. There was a 75% reduction in the storage of materials for work in progress, which led to an 8% reduction of distance traveled. With less material on the floor, they were able to move the workstations closer together reducing the distance traveled. The rate in which employees process the material through the plant improved by 213% and they were 54% more productive.

The labor savings, over a six-month period, has been approximately $54,000 in the DCMI production alone. The remainder of the departments will have a Kaizen event during 2000, which will yield savings in other cells.

Source: *New Jersey Manufacturing Extension Program Inc.* (www)

The New Jersey Manufacturing Extension Program Inc. (NJMEP) is a not-for-profit organisation charged with assisting New Jersey's small and medium-sized manufacturers to become more productive, profitable and globally competitive – www.njmep.org

For more about lean manufacturing, try searching the Internet using the key words 'lean manufacturing'. You will find a lot of applications of lean thinking.

Continuous improvement is a typical TQM approach as some of the key words and phrases of TQM frequently occur when the subject is raised – such as involvement, cascading to all levels of the organisation, teamwork, quality tools (concepts), product quality and commitment from the top. However, it can be used in isolation from TQM, for example when managers implement continuous improvement at team level.

The PDCA cycle

Continuous improvement, a never-ending process, is often portrayed as a cycle of repeated activities. TQM guru W E Deming invented a way of demonstrating this, called the PDCA cycle or Deming wheel. PDCA stands for Plan, Do, Check, Act – see Figure 2.2.

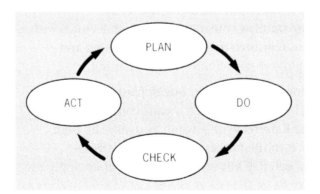

Figure 2.2 *The PDCA cycle*

The cycle starts with the **plan** stage, which involves an investigation and analysis of the problem area, followed by the **do** or implementation stage, where the plan is tried out in operation. Next is the **check** or monitoring stage, which involves evaluating the results against expectations, and finally the **act** or consolidation stage, where the change is standardised or lessons are learned from the experience. Then the cycle starts again.

You can find a number of sites on the Internet which deal exclusively with continuous improvement, such as www.kaizen-institute.com – a global management consultancy specialising in continuous improvement tools and strategies. It features Masaaki Imai's follow-up to his best-selling book *Kaizen: The Key to Japan's Competitive Success* (1986), called Gemba Kaizen: A Commonsense, Low-Cost Approach to Management (1997).

Activity 5
Kaizen

Objective

This activity asks you to identify the key ingredients of *kaizen*.

Case study

Read the case study and complete the task that follows.

Kaizen is a CD hit

In an organization, Kaizen is a team concept that means continuous and incremental improvement at all levels. Machine operator, middle manager, even the CEO are part of the process. The Kaizen umbrella covers the famous manufacturing techniques such as just-in-time inventory, zero defects, quality circles, and suggestion systems. They're all components of the continuous improvement philosophy.

Basically, you take a look at your operations and you eliminate everything that's wasteful. In Kaizen circles, we use the Japanese word for waste, which is 'muda.' Muda means all those things you do that don't add value. It's the deadly enemy of value creation. The eight deadly muda are waste of motion, time delays, unnecessary transporting and material handling, making defects, overprocessing, overproducing, storing inventory, and missed opportunity. If you can drive that kind of waste out of your process and stay vigilant about it, then you've reached the heart of Kaizen. Here's where the art of standardization becomes your friend. You have to rigorously standardize your processes if you are going to rigorously improve them.

Maintaining your best processes and improving them involves two key activities, what we call two cycle wheels. The first cycle is for maintaining your best processes, which is the day-to-day concern of operators and technicians. The other is the improvement cycle, which is generally the responsibility of the management and engineering staffs. Management and technical staff have the lead responsibility for introducing improvements to the standardization processes. But they don't act in a vacuum. They spend the majority of their time on the factory floor, measuring compliance with the Kaizen-driven plan, looking at the manufacturing process from the individual perspective of each employee.

We do it with fewer employees. Yet we have not laid off any workers. Our head count has dropped from a high of about 1500 employees to our current status of just under 1000, all through attrition. Kaizen improves the morale of our employees by removing drudgery from work and developing pride in seeing individual ideas implemented.

With the emphasis on automation, cycle time on the CD lines has been drastically driven down in this process. Gone, for example, are the batch process lines of the late 1980s. The Terre Haute plant, which Sony purchased from CBS in 1983, makes discs faster than anybody in the world. Automatic guided vehicles carry supplies and discs from one station to another. Everything is automated, from retrieving manufacturing supplies to the manufacturing process itself; even the stacking of packed boxes of discs on a pallet for shipping.

Source: *Mitchell and Fairbanks* (2000)

Task

Make a list of the key ingredients of *kaizen* from Sony's point of view.

Sony's key ingredients of kaizen:

Feedback

Here's our list of *kaizen's* key ingredients from Sony's point of view:

- involvement at all levels
- just-in-time inventory
- zero defects
- quality circles
- suggestion systems
- elimination of waste – the eight deadly *muda*
- improvements to standardization processes (from the employee's point of view)
- measuring compliance with the *kaizen*-driven plan
- reduced employee headcount
- improvement in employee morale by removing drudgery from work and developing pride in seeing individual ideas implemented
- quicker cycle time
- automation.

You may like to discuss with your colleagues whether you could implement similar ideas in your work area/organisation. What areas would benefit?

Improvement tools and techniques

Mankind thus inevitably sets itself only such tasks as it is able to solve, since closer examination will always show that the problem itself arises only when the material conditions for its solution are already present or at least in the course of formation.

Source: *Marx* (1859)

Much of the concern over improvement concerns problem solving. How can we get costs down? How can we eliminate waste? How can we get down to zero defects? Why are customers dissatisfied with the service we provide? Why is our supply chain so unreliable? Why aren't we getting any benefits from our IT system?

TQM specifically provides tools for problem solving and making quality improvements.

Flow charts

Flow charts present a detailed, visual explanation of the flow in a process. They can be used to find blockages in a process or to develop new processes.

They are useful as design documents and as historical documents that show the way a process works. They can be revisited if a process needs to be developed. Flow charts consist of **actions** which appear in rectangular boxes and **yes and no decisions** which appear in diamond-shaped boxes (though there are other symbols you can use). They are connected by **flow lines**.

Slack et al. (2001) give an example of a flow chart (shown in Figure 2.3) which was used by Kaston Pyral Services Ltd – a field-service division of Kaston Pyral International which manufactures and installs gas-fired heating systems – to improve its customer query service. The question marks indicate that there is a problem here as there are areas where no actions are being taken, in this case identified as information not being recorded.

As a result of this flow chart, Kaston Pyral Services decided to log all customer queries so that it could analyse customer problems more closely.

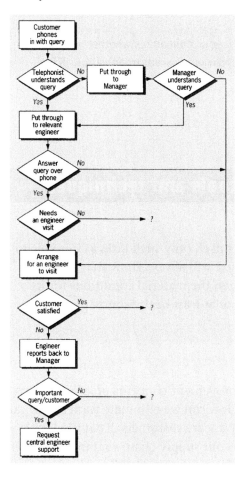

Figure 2.3 *Flow chart for customer query at Kaston Pyral Services*

Source: *Slack et al.* (2001)

Look up www.flowcharts.com for more about flow charts.

Scatter diagrams

Scatter diagrams are used to establish an association, connection or correlation between two sets of variable data.

A typical X/Y graph is drawn, points are plotted based on observations and conclusions can be drawn from the way the points are spread – see Figure 2.4 which shows scatter diagrams used by Kaston Pyral Services. The closer, more linear the plots, the closer the relationship, and vice versa.

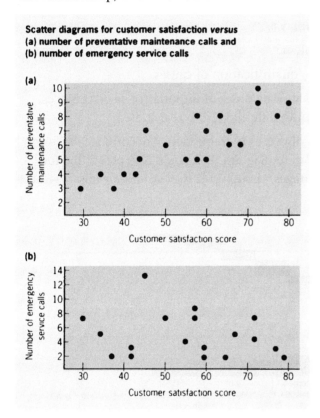

Figure 2.4 *Scatter diagrams at Kaston Pyral Services*

Source: *Slack et al.* (2001)

The first scatter diagram (a) shows a clear relationship between customer satisfaction and number of call-outs – try drawing a straight line between the plots. The dots in the second diagram (b) are all over the place, showing little correlation between the factors, so it suggests customer satisfaction is not affected by, or improved by, more emergency visits. As a result of the second analysis, the company decided to survey customers' views on its emergency service.

Note that scatter diagrams only identify whether there is a relationship, or not, between factors. They do not necessarily imply cause and effect. This can be shown later via a cause and effect diagram.

Pareto analysis

Pareto analysis is named after the 19th-century Italian economist Vilfredo Pareto who noticed that 80 per cent of the wealth of his country was owned by 20 per cent of the population (Pareto's law).

In the 20th century, this led to the Pareto diagram which is essentially a bar chart which prioritises the causes of a problem based on the concept that 80 per cent of the problem is attributable to 20 per cent of the causes. In other words, it separates the significant few from the trivial many. Hence the usefulness of Pareto analysis is that it enables organisations to focus on area(s) which will give the greatest improvement(s).

To carry out Pareto analysis:

1   Identify your problem.

2   Collect your data – quantification of causes.

3   Rank causes in descending order of importance as percentages. Cumulative percentages should also be calculated.

4   Plot an X/Y graph of causes to frequency of occurrence (%) using a bar chart – the Pareto diagram. You could also plot a line for cumulative percentages, though this isn't strictly necessary – see Figure 2.5.

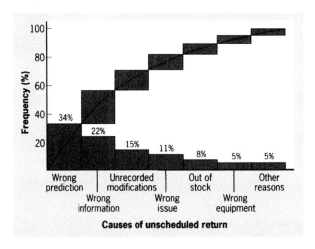

Figure 2.5 *Pareto diagram at Kaston Pyral Services*   Source: *Slack et al.* (2001)

Figure 2.5 shows a diagram for unscheduled returns from emergency servicing at Kaston Pyral Services. As you can see, the first two categories are the significant few.

As a result of this analysis, the company decided to concentrate on how to get more information to its engineers to enable them to make a more accurate diagnosis of the job. This could be achieved by telephonist training, more accurate customer records, customer system modifications, etc.

Cause and effect diagrams

If you want to establish cause and effect when problem solving, then a good tool is the cause and effect diagram. This visual tool was invented by TQM guru Kaoru Ishikawa. It is also known as the Ishikawa diagram – after its inventor – or the fishbone diagram because it looks like a fish's skeleton. The general appearance of the cause and effect diagram is shown in Figure 2.6.

The idea is to use brainstorming or group discussion to identify the problem, the main causes and the sub-causes, and to record these by constructing a cause and effect diagram using a large sheet of paper. The effect is placed at the end of the 'backbone' – this is the problem you are analysing. The main causes – sometimes broken down into machinery, manpower, materials, methods and money – are listed on each of the 'ribs'. These can then be broken down into any number of sub-causes. Hang as many bones on the skeleton as possible, as at this stage it is really a question of identifying **potential** causes. Then, through further analysis, circle the main causes of the problem (effect) and there you have your cause and effect diagram.

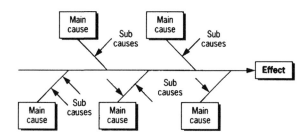

Figure 2.6 *The basic structure of a cause and effect diagram*

Figure 2.7 is an example of a cause and effect diagram created at Hewlett-Packard to identify why so many defective toner cartridges were being returned to the company.

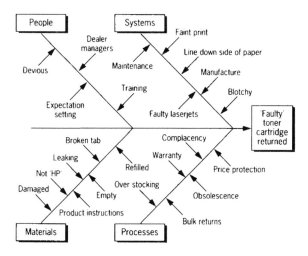

Figure 2.7 *Cause and effect diagram at Hewlett-Packard*

Source: *adapted from Slack et al. (2001)*

In the event, Hewlett-Packard identified the following reasons for the problem:

- Some people couldn't load the toner cartridge properly or deal with minor problems that arose

- Some dealers couldn't sort out minor problems

- Some toner cartridges were being sent to unauthorised refilling companies, which were refilling the same cartridges up to five times so they were wearing out, and the toner in the refilled cartridges was not up to Hewlett-Packard's normal standards.

As a result of this analysis, Hewlett-Packard tightened up its returns policy and improved its instructions to customers on how to use its products. Complaints in all areas shrank to a fraction of what they had previously been.

Activity 6
Improvement tools and techniques – cause and effect diagrams

Objective

Use this activity to analyse a problem using a cause and effect diagram.

Task

1 Think of a problem in your work area that you would like to get to the bottom of, so that you can understand and prioritise the main causes. Plan to work with your team in a group session to investigate this problem.

2 Write the problem or issue in a box on the right-hand side of a whiteboard or flip chart. This is the 'head' of the fish in the diagram. Then draw the 'spine' and main 'ribs' of the fish.

3 Ask, 'What is causing this problem?' Write each possible cause at the end of each rib. Alternatively, use broad categories for the main causes, such as people, policy, procedures, methods, machinery, materials.

4 Focus on each main cause in turn and ask, 'What contributes to this cause?' or 'What are the issues behind this cause?' and note each new sub-cause on a line coming off the fish's rib.

5 Examine the completed diagram to find relationships between the causes and sub-causes. You may find one issue comes up repeatedly. This will help you to identify some of the most important likely causes.

6 Decide what action you should take now. Do you need to carry out further investigation to find out which causes are most significant? What action can you take to minimise or get rid of any of the causes?

Feedback

You should find that by setting out the problem diagrammatically, you can break it down into its many causes and then look at it as a whole. It should enable you to identify whether more information is needed, or it could give you enough information to make changes that get rid of some of the causes you feel are significant.

If you need to investigate the causes further by collecting data about them, you may be able to identify the most significant causes using a Pareto chart. This uses a bar chart to show the frequency of each cause (so it tends to work when quantifiable data on a cause can be collected). The idea is that you will normally find that 80 per cent of the problem can be attributable to 20 per cent of the causes.

You will find that improvement tools can only help you to find your way through a problem. Unfortunately they don't provide the answers.

Employee involvement

Employee involvement is about the greater participation of employees in work-based tasks, both for individual and group-based working. Securing greater involvement in the tasks an individual performs is said to increase job satisfaction, strengthen morale, increase commitment and improve quality.

Europe: Teamworking is Key to Company Success
Many businesses that are thriving adopt a business approach that is all about teamwork. High performing companies, such as Hewlett-Packard and Richard Branson's Virgin Group use this method. Groups, or teams, of workers are employed, working together to solve issues. In this manner, the employer gets the best out of his/her workforce and tends to attract highly intelligent people who do not feel restricted by heavy-handed management. Teamwork is said to be the way forward for

companies in the EU, who are already behind America and Japan.

Source: *Irish Times* (2000)

Quality Drives Trident's Success

Trident Precision Manufacturing's people-oriented total quality management (TQM) initiative is behind the financial success of this precision sheet-metal fabricator and electromechanical assembly company. The TQM program entailed that managers participate in the recruitment process to demonstrate the interest of managers in their people right from the start. In addition, employees were trained on TQM tools by the HR [human resources] department to teach them to make decisions on their own and therefore empower them to solve problems that crop up without having to rely on superiors. Their achievements are recognized annually, not just once but a number of times through different memorabilia items. Finally, the HR department measures progress in terms of productivity as well as customer satisfaction. The result is the quadrupling of revenue within a 10-year period, reduction of turnover and increase of employee productivity.

Source: *Laabs* (1998)

Job redesign

Job redesign is about restructuring the job to make it more interesting, motivating and involving. It should also make it more productive. There are four main types of job redesign:

- ◆ Job enrichment – this involves altering the job so that there is task variety, task significance, autonomy, and a feedback mechanism available, for example, where operators on an assembly line take responsibility for basic maintenance operations and record keeping.

- ◆ Job enlargement – this is similar to job enrichment but emphasises task variety, namely extending the number of tasks an employee does, like bus drivers who hand out tickets as well.

- ◆ Job rotation – here employees move about from one job to another so that they can eventually perform all the jobs in a process. For example, as a hotel undermanager, you would have to spend some time in the kitchen, some time on the front desk, in the back office, on the bar, etc.

- ◆ Teamworking – this is where groups work together for a common purpose and with shared accountability. While some teams are structured to be managed or led by a team leader, others are autonomous and its members make all the main decisions themselves for defined tasks. The idea of teamworking began in the 1950s and 1960s and autonomous work groups became common in car and other manufacturing plants. Philips, the electrical equipment manufacturer, pioneered teamworking and Volvo introduced it in the 1970s and 1980s, though in the end found it was too costly.

Not everyone agrees about the efficacy of job redesign. It has shown some good results – it can improve productivity, reduce employee turnover, cut wastage costs and improve quality – but there have also been criticisms that it asks too much of individuals. Teamworking in particular can be quite stressful for those involved. Again, if reward structures do not keep pace with greater accountabilities, dissatisfaction will increase rather than dissipate.

Quality circles

Quality circles are also a form of employee involvement but are important enough within TQM to be considered in their own right. Quality circles are voluntary work groups who meet regularly – perhaps for an hour or so once a fortnight – to discuss how to improve the quality of products and work processes. They are essentially **problem-solving** groups. They arose in Japan where they have been very successful, but they have not been as successful in the West. This is perhaps because the conditions in which they arose in Japan – large percentage of the workforce in quality circles, extensive training in quality measurement concepts and high level of trust between management and employees – were not prevalent in the West at the time. They have since come under pressure from new concepts such as quality improvement teams and task force or tiger teams.

Outdoing the hackers
Imagine a team of people spending all their time thinking up ways of hacking into corporate computer networks. Now imagine them, Mission Impossible-style, breaking into the inner sanctum itself – the main computer room. These teams actually exist and, more remarkably, they work largely from within the big firms of accountants. Known as 'tiger teams', their brief is to find the holes in the security of their corporate clients before criminal hackers do.

Brick trick
Jan Babiak is head of Ernst & Young's IT security practice. She told me how one of her firm's tiger teams broke into the

computer room of a major North American client, deposited a brick marked 'Ernst & Young was here' and left again undetected. They then contacted the firm's bosses and said: 'Come and see what we've done.' What a great job, don't you think? Kind of James Bond without the disincentive of being shot at. But, of course, it's not quite as simple as that. Most of the time, the teams are methodically trying to crack passwords to find a chink in the armour of supposedly secure sites.

Chris Potter, partner in charge of similar operations at PricewaterhouseCoopers, said his 50-strong UK team mainly tries to replicate the techniques of illegal hackers to probe here and there until weaknesses are identified. Physical break-ins would be rare, he said, and used only when the client had agreed it was appropriate.

Jan Babiak also stressed the importance of not being alarmist: 'The smartest thing to do is to understand your risks.' Then, she said, you can develop cost-effective responses that deal with the risk in a way that 'delivers good value to shareholders'. Now there's the accountant speaking.

Source: *Rodger* (2000)

Steps to problem solving in quality circles

A typical problem-solving process using quality circles is as follows:

1 Quality circle forms and meets.

2 Members select problems and projects they wish to tackle.

3 Members generate solutions and evaluate them at another meeting, particularly looking at cost-effectiveness.

4 Recommendations go to senior management for approval.

5 Quality circle implements solutions when approved.

6 Quality circle monitors solutions by gaining feedback from operators.

7 Quality circle makes a review of solutions to generate improvements.

T&D and quality

Training and development (T&D) and learning are a key aspect of the quality argument. One of the failures of TQM occurs when T&D is not carried out correctly, is not extensive or does not cover subject areas in enough depth, is unfocused, is inadequately resourced or is ad hoc rather than continuous. For example, as noted above, quality circles have been largely unsuccessful in the West because of the failure to carry out the type of training needed to get across the concepts involved.

What sort of T&D is required?

This depends on how much quality management you want and in what areas. The list below is a typical selection of T&D subject areas that encompass TQM:

- problem-solving skills
- teamworking and team leadership skills
- improvement and control tools and techniques
- understanding wastage and costs
- process control
- maintenance
- training in quality systems and standards (mandatory for ISO 9000)
- training in TQM concepts and principles
- customer-care training
- communication and information skills
- cultural change programme
- health, safety and environment training
- continuous improvement or *kaizen* training
- training for new skills as a result of job redesign.

Training must be accompanied by ongoing projects to practise what is learned. For TQM it should encompass everyone from the Chief Executive Officer (CEO) to temporary employees. It should be reinforced by further training because some of the concepts and skills take time to sink in.

Activity 7
You and your team

Objective

Use this activity to evaluate ideas for greater employee involvement in your own organisation.

Task

Complete the following chart of ideas for employee involvement by assessing how useful each idea is for your work area/organisation. Think about the following in making your assessment:

- ◆ Would they improve the way you work now?
- ◆ Are they appropriate or relevant to the way your work is structured and/or your organisational culture?
- ◆ What would be the benefits for you and your organisation of a change?
- ◆ What would be the costs, and do these costs outweigh the benefits?
- ◆ If you already use some of these ideas, re-evaluate their usefulness in the light of your experience.

Employee involvement ideas	*How useful for my work area/organisation*
Job enrichment	
Job enlargement	
Job rotation	
Teamworking	
Quality circles	
Training in quality concepts and practices	

Feedback

As we mentioned previously, not everyone agrees about the efficacy of job redesign. It has shown some good results – it can improve productivity, reduce employee turnover, cut wastage costs and improve quality – but there have also been criticisms that it asks too much of individuals. Teamworking, in particular, can be quite stressful for those involved. If reward structures do not keep pace with greater accountabilities, dissatisfaction will increase rather than dissipate. Teamworking may not be appropriate to the type of work your organisation does or to the way you work. For example, the type of role culture/structure typically seen in banks or the civil service, where management likes to control in a hierarchical way, is not conducive to people working autonomously.

Talk about your answers for this activity with your team. What do the team members think?

◆ Recap

Identify your customers and how to gain feedback on their needs and expectations

- ◆ Internal customers are a key part of your organisation's supply chain and as such are as important as the ultimate customer or consumer for your organisation's products or services.

- ◆ Suppliers are also customers in the sense that they need to know what you want from them.

Consider approaches to quality improvement and how you can apply them to the products or services you provide

- ◆ There are two approaches to improvement of processes, products, and services: continuous (incremental, small steps) and breakthrough (giant step) actions.

- ◆ The plan-do-check-act cycle provides a framework that you can apply for continuous improvement of products and services.

Explore a range of analytical tools and techniques for problem solving and quality improvement

- ◆ Quality tools can help you to identify problems and to analyse their cause.

- ◆ Flow charts, scatter diagrams, Pareto analysis, and cause and effect diagrams are all examples of quality tools.

Consider how you can involve your team in improving quality and customer service

- ◆ Empowering involves delegating responsibility to people to make decisions and take action. Effective teamwork, communication, and training and development are critical if people are to operate effectively in an empowered environment.

- ◆ Quality circles are problem solving groups of individuals who are empowered to identify and solve problems in the operating environment.

►► More @

Peters, T. and Waterman, R. (1982) *In Search of Excellence,* HarperCollins

In what was to become one of the best-selling business books of all time, Tom Peters challenged the systems approach to business success and focused instead on people, customers and action as the key differentiators of business excellence.

Brown, S., Blackmon, K., Cousins, P, and Maylor, H. (2001) *Operations Management,* **Butterworth-Heinemann**
This comprehensive text provides cutting-edge input into operations management theory and practice and has sections dedicated to performance management and improvement.

The **DTI** website provides a guide to improvement at www.dti.gov.uk/bestpractice/operations/quality.htm

Huffman, J. L. (1997) *Beyond TQM: Tools & Techniques for High Performance Improvement,* **Lanchester Press**
Try this book for more about improvement tools and techniques

The **Kaisen Institute** at www.kaizen-institute.com is just one of a number of consultancy organisations specialising in, and providing resources on, continuous improvement tools and strategies

3   Operations management

This theme focuses on quality in an operations context. It shows how you, as a manager, can add value to the processes that you manage by adopting operations management practices. In particular, you explore two aspects of operations management:

- Design – both the design of products and services you supply and the design of the operational processes used to create and deliver them.

- Planning and control – how you manage those operational processes on a day-to-day basis so that you are able to fulfil customer demand.

You will:

- **Define operations management and identify five performance measures for quality operations**

- **Explore processes for designing products, services and operational processes that meet business goals**

- **Identify key activities and issues in planning and control**

- **Examine two techniques for the measurement and control of operations.**

Quality in operations

What are operations?

As far as organisations are concerned, operations are those transformation processes which convert inputs to outputs – see Figure 3.1.

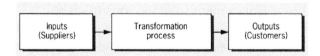

Figure 3.1 *The organisation as a transformation process: operations*

The following definitions apply to the model:

- Inputs – labour, materials, capital, data (resources)

- Transformation processes – business operations and production processes

- Outputs – goods, services, profits and wages, information (products).

> **High-quality operations do not waste time having to re-do things.**

All organisations have operations of some sort or other. That is the purpose of the organisation – to use operations to produce goods and services. They don't have to be goods or manufacturing operations; they can be information or service operations – see Table 3.1.

Organisation	Inputs	Transformation processes	Outputs
Online insurance provider	IT staff, Web investment, insurance and risk assessment expertise	Selling insurance over Internet	Insurance policies
Microsoft plc	Code, data, IT skills, reinvesting, high-tech offices	Programming, Web development	Software, MSN (Web portal)
Local football team	Kit, players, equipment, pitch	Training, playing games, scoring goals	Goals, championship, cups
British Airways (BA)	Pilots, planes, groundcrew, passengers, freight, data	Selling tickets, flying people and materials from one place to another, processing schedule data	Tickets sent out, people/ materials transported to destination, travel information
Tesco	Employees, wholesale goods, supermarkets, website	Selling retail goods and services, giving customer service	Products taken away by customers, customer queries answered

Table 3.1 *Different types of operations processes*

Figure 3.1 is a simple model. Of course, at any one time, an organisation may have hundreds or thousands of operations going on – large or small – from answering a telephone enquiry to landing an aircraft. It is the planning and control of these operations that are the concern of operations management.

What is operations management?

Operations management is about carrying out those activities which ensure products and services go through the transformation process – from design, through production to delivery. It's really the core activity of most managers, particularly line managers, though it may not be called operations management in service organisations. Managers may have other activities with which they are concerned, such as people management, budgeting or IT development – and in many organisations they will be separate functions – but these are support activities whereas operations management is considered to be a core activity. Figure 3.2 explains this point in terms of management functions.

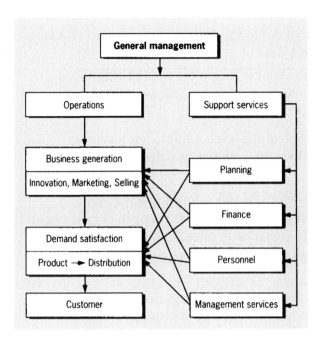

Figure 3.2 *Management operations and support functions*

Source: *Armstrong* (1990)

Operations managers translate operational strategy into design and planning and control processes, but they are also concerned with improving performance in these processes – this is where quality comes into the equation.

The quality operation

Quality is one of the key performance objectives by which an operation can be evaluated. Slack et al. (2001) note five performance objectives:

- quality – doing things right
- speed – doing things fast
- dependability – doing things on time
- flexibility – being able to change what you do
- cost – doing things cheaply.

Quality and Operations concentrates on quality, but quality is intertwined with the other objectives. In the section 'What is quality?' we made the point about the value-based approach to quality which concentrates on prices and costs. In other words, you can't really have quality if operational costs are high and prices scare customers away. Flexibility, speed and dependability can also be seen as quality issues – and indeed they can also be seen as cost issues.

Each of the performance objectives has several internal effects, but all of them affect cost:

♦ High quality operations do not waste time or effort having to re-do things, nor are their internal customers inconvenienced by flawed service.

♦ Fast operations reduce the level of in-process inventory between micro-operations, as well as reducing administrative overheads.

♦ Dependable operations do not spring any unwelcome surprises on their internal customers. They can be relied upon to deliver exactly as planned. This eliminates wasteful disruption and allows the other micro-operations to operate efficiently.

♦ Flexible operations adapt to changing circumstances quickly and without disrupting the rest of the operation. Flexible micro-operations can also change over between tasks quickly and without wasting time and capacity.

Inside the operation, therefore, one important way to improve cost performance is to improve the performance of the other operations objectives.

Source: *Slack et al.* (2001)

Quality, speed, dependability, flexibility and cost run through the whole operations management process. They are applicable as much to design as to planning and control. The remaining sections will explore these points further.

Activity 8
Quality in operations

Objective

This activity will help you to assess how to make quality improvements in operations.

Case study

Read the case study and complete the task that follows.

VelQuest Announces Collaboration with AstraZeneca: Opening the Door to a Paperless Laboratory Environment

VelQuest, a leading provider of Electronic Process Management and Compliance technology, ePMC™, to the heavily regulated life-science environment, including pharmaceutical development, quality operations, manufacturing, generic pharmaceuticals, biotechnology companies and contract analytical laboratories, and AstraZeneca, a worldwide leading pharmaceutical provider, announced today that they are implementing VelQuest's ePMC solution.

VelQuest's ePMC solution was chosen as the best approach for the project because the solution enables quality controlled automated data-collection from networked laboratory instruments, and it facilitates prompt and easy retrieval of process data from a centrally located database. VelQuest's innovative and proprietary ePMC solution promotes the collection of quality data by linking data-collection to standard operating procedures and provides a complete history for all process data. Furthermore, the VelQuest ePMC solution serves recent FDA regulations, specifically Rule 21 CFR Part 11, governing the use of electronic records and signatures in FDA regulated research, manufacturing and clinical facilities.

'A critical challenge faced by pharmaceutical companies is increasing productivity without sacrificing process control and compliance standards,' said Michael Stroz, Sr. Manager of Analytical at AstraZeneca's Westborough, MA Production facility. 'After studying this sector in detail, we believe VelQuest's solution will reduce time for reviewers by 50 per cent, liberate over 20 per cent of our overall lab operations staff, and create an electronic compliance platform for today and the future.'

'This collaboration is a significant step towards solving critical pharmaceutical development and quality operations resource challenges. Our research concluded that up to 70 per cent of staff in these areas are devoted to paper-based, compliance-driven activities. Creating a real-time electronic laboratory compliance platform will help companies liberate resources, reduce quality control release times, and enable our customers to bring important new human therapeutics to the market more rapidly,' stated Ken Rapp, VelQuest Corporation's President and CEO.

Source: *Business Wire* (2001b)

Task

What quality improvements does AstraZeneca hope to make in its operations as a result of adopting VelQuest's ePMC™ solution?

The improvements AstraZeneca hope to make:

Feedback

Your list of quality improvements that AstraZeneca expects from VelQuest's ePMC™ solution could include:

◆ prompt and easy retrieval of process data

◆ linking of data collection to standard operating procedures

◆ provision of a complete history for all process data

◆ compliance with electronic data requirements applying to the industry

◆ productivity improvements through reducing reviewer's time, freeing up human and material resources, reducing quality control release times and speeding up the delivery of new products to the market.

Better by design

Operations management starts with design. Unless you design, and design well, later planning and control will be hampered by the limitations built into your products and services and operations processes.

The French TGV (*Train à Grande Vitesse*) is the fastest train in the world with a world record speed of 320.3 mph and a regular speed of 186 mph. It incorporates new product design features in aerodynamics, coupling, power supply, braking and computerised signalling. It has also set new standards of design in comfort, convenience, safety and the environment. However, its performance on cost – tracks and signalling estimated at $33 million per mile to build – is less impressive.

The design of products and services is a process involving a number of sequential or concurrent stages. Typically, they include the following:

1 Developing a concept – a concept is generated from the ideas that people have. These can be ideas from customers, suppliers, staff, marketing research or from benchmarking competitors – for example, using suggestion schemes to involve employees.

2 Making an initial design – this involves specifying the components and processes involved in the concept – for example, to design a new car you would have to specify the material components, visual design elements, manufacturing processes, and so on.

3 Creating a prototype – this is a working model of the finished product to test the design. It may be a clay or plastic model, or even a virtual prototype such as a computer-aided design (CAD) model.

4 Agreeing a specification – after various testings and evaluations, a final specification is agreed.

Evaluation, testing, screening, etc. are constant and occur throughout the design process. Typical design evaluation and testing techniques include:

♦ Taguchi methods – a statistical approach to test the robustness of a design in extreme conditions

♦ failure mode and effect analysis (FMEA) – a risk-assessment technique involving likelihood, consequence and detectability of product failure

♦ quality function deployment (QFD) – a technique to ensure the eventual design of a product or service meets the needs of its customers. See the following case study.

Customer and supplier involvement

A key aspect of designing products and services – and one which brings out the quality issue – is to involve customers and suppliers in the design evaluation process. For example, quality function deployment is often used in manufacturing to ensure that the eventual design of a product meets the needs/expectations of customers.

The following case study illustrates how customers and suppliers (vendors) can be involved in the design process to enhance quality.

Quality
At TVS Suzuki, the quality process runs right through New Product Development to aftersales service. Our New Product Development (NPD) process begins with Quality Function

Deployment (QFD) where identified customer requirements are clearly defined and stated. Consequently, any variance between this customer-demanded quality versus resultant-design quality are thoroughly analysed and necessary improvements are made at various stages of NPD.

Reduction in the New Product Development (NPD) cycle time is achieved through concurrent engineering which involves all relevant internal departments and their vendors.

This group collectively analyses and approves the process feasibility and thereby determines further product development. The Failure Mode Effect Analysis (FMEA) process is carried out on new products to ensure their reliability. Product or prototype testing is conducted through accelerated testing processes. Thus, product quality is assessed at the prototype stage itself.

Source: *TVS Suzuki Ltd* (www)

Concurrent (simultaneous) engineering

The use of concurrent engineering in the previous case study is a good example of design practices that improve quality. Concurrent engineering means that design processes can carry on simultaneously without the need to wait for one stage to end before another begins. This:

♦ reduces time taken to get the product to market

♦ enables more features to be incorporated in the product at less cost

♦ produces more new products more often.

See *www.dti.gov.uk/mbp for more information.*

Designing operational processes

Design is not just about the product or service being developed. A number of other factors are important in the design process. These include:

♦ process technology
♦ network design
♦ layout and flow
♦ job design.

Process technology

It's no good designing a new product if you don't have some idea of the technology you are going to use to manufacture it. The next case study illustrates this point.

'World first' for plastic

MCP Equipment of Stone, Staffordshire, believes its MCP 50/E blowmoulding machine is the world's first to be specifically designed for the production of prototype plastic bottles and containers.

Launched at Pakex, the machine can be installed within design facilities alongside benchtop vacuum casting machines and other rapid prototyping equipment.

Quality prototype bottles and containers in capacities up to one litre can be made quickly for trials in PE, PP, HDPE and ABS. MCP's EP250 Rapid Prototype Tooling System allows the production of tools from a rapid prototype model in less than one week.

Source: *Packaging Magazine* (2001)

Process technology is the machines and equipment you intend to use to create and deliver your new products and services – you need to identify what the machine/equipment needs to do to produce the required product. Technology can range from a lathe to bar code scanners to the complex robotic technology that is used in car manufacture. It also includes information technology such as expert systems for capacity planning and inventory (stock) control, database applications for customer feedback, and the Internet for product and service delivery.

Network design

The operations network refers to the people who will interface with any new product or service, namely customers and suppliers. It is about the design of the supply chain and should involve considerations of location and capacity. For example, many Japanese companies located parts of their operations to the UK in the 1990s to take advantage of tax breaks, favourable currency rates and low labour costs. New car models were specifically developed with these locations in mind. The UK location was also suitable for ease of access to the greater European market.

Layout and flow

This refers to the physical way an operation is laid out. For example, in the previous case study about MCP Equipment of Stone, Staffordshire, it says:

> Launched at Pakex, the machine can be installed within design facilities alongside benchtop vacuum casting machines and other rapid prototyping equipment.

This is a direct reference to the way the operation will work in terms of layout and flow.

Imagine the design of a new store. The way the equipment, floorwalking space, fixtures and fittings, partitions, etc. are laid out is directly relevant to the store merchandising requirements. For example, having an escalator in the front entrance does not give a good overview of the store and may be off-putting to customers.

Safety, flexibility, comfort, accessibility and co-ordination may also be relevant where, say, people are working on assembly lines to produce new products.

Layout and flow also includes the sequencing of the operation in terms of what parts of the operation follow on from other parts. Flow charts could be used to help to determine this.

Job design

Job design refers to the way a job is carried out in terms of its tasks, duties and responsibilities, including interaction with equipment, the environment and other people.

> Inadequate attention to the job design of telephonists selling products, providing customer service and answering customer queries in call centres has led to high turnover of employees in the UK. The problem is that telephonists are like battery hens attached to their kiosks for long hours, performing demanding, repetitive operations in relatively cramped conditions. This has led to stress and job dissatisfaction.

The way people interface with their job has safety and environmental implications as well as behavioural ones. Ergonomics is the study of the physiological aspects of work. Incorrect attention to ergonomics can affect employees' health – for example, repetitive strain injury for those working too long at computers, vibration white finger for those using drilling equipment without adequate safeguards, loss of hearing for those working in excessively noisy work areas.

There is a clear link to quality with job design.

Other operational processes

These are not the only processes the operations designer could consider. A number of other factors link in with the processes described above, such as:

- quantity and continuity of products required – for example mass production, jobbing production (small orders), batch production (intermittent orders) or one-off projects

- work organisation – for example, the degree of automation, shift working, flexible working, group working and scheduling.

Activity 9
Design in operations

Objective

Use this activity to draw a flow chart for a work process.

Task

Use a separate piece of paper for this task.

1 Consider a recent new development in your work area, or one to come, which altered or will alter the way you work. If you can't think of a new one, consider a process that is fundamental to your work objectives.

2 Draw a flow chart that shows how you interact, or will interact, with the new development or process – what activities you have to carry out and decisions you have to make. Figure 3.3 overleaf shows an example for health and safety design.

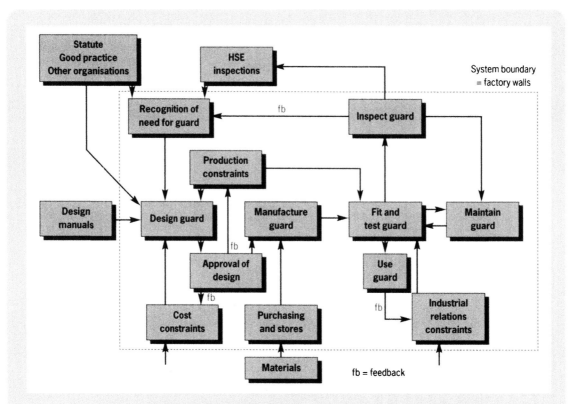

Figure 3.3 *Systems diagram of the provision of a guard* Source: *Ridley* (1994)

3 Check that your flow chart is accurate by testing it. Then consider whether you can find ways to improve your contribution to the process. Would it help if you made your contribution earlier or later? Do you need more or different information in order to contribute effectively?

Feedback

You may want to discuss the implications of your flow chart with work colleagues.

Does the process need to be changed? How feasible is this?

Operations planning and control

Operations planning and control follows operations design because once a product/service has been designed, it needs to be produced. Operations planning and control is concerned with ensuring that the day-to-day production process proceeds smoothly.

Quality is an important part of this process as quality should be one of the key performance objectives against which any operation is measured, but quality can go further than this. The integration of quality processes, systems and techniques into operations planning and control can ensure that the whole process is quality based.

Planning and control activities

Operational planning is an estimation of what needs to be done to ensure operational processes are efficient and effective – that supply always meets demand. Operational control is to ensure that operations conform with this estimation, and if they do not, adjustments can be made.

Typical activities in the planning and control process include:

- setting objectives – so that you know what is to be achieved by your plans and by when

- allocating tasks and responsibilities – who is to be involved with the new product and service and how they are to be involved

- scheduling – work patterns, process scheduling, supply and demand scheduling

- assessing resource requirements – people and their skills, money (budgets), time, raw materials, plant and equipment, capacity

- monitoring and evaluating performance – the control part, involving control activities, measures and control techniques.

Push and pull control

Controlling operations is about ensuring that operations go according to plan by monitoring, intervention and correction. There are two main types of control in terms of periodic intervention into product operations (see Figure 3.4):

- Push control – this is where control activities are scheduled by means of a central system and completed in line with central instructions, as in materials requirements planning (MRP). Work is pushed from one stage to another regardless of whether it is needed. This can result in queues, idle time and inventory build up.

♦ Pull control – this is where work is only passed to the next stage in the process when that stage asks for it. This is demand-led as opposed to the supply-led approach of push control systems, for example, as in just-in-time (JIT) operations.

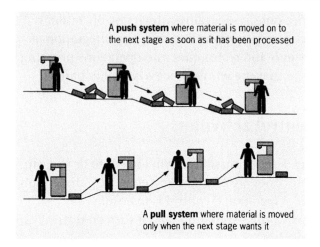

A **push system** where material is moved on to the next stage as soon as it has been processed

A **pull system** where material is moved only when the next stage wants it

Figure 3.4 *Push and pull control*   Source: *Slack et al.* (2001)

Quality planning and control

Quality planning and control means putting into place those systems, standards, processes and techniques which ensure the operations process will be quality based. It involves using performance objectives against which operations can be measured.

Quality control and performance measures

Slack et al. (2001) note a number of ways to measure operations performance objectives – see Table 3.2. Any of these performance indicators can measure performance in the areas mentioned. They can also be measurements of quality.

Performance objective	Some typical performance measures (indicators)
Quality	Number of defects per unit Level of customer complaints Scrap level Warranty claims Mean time between failures Customer satisfaction score
Speed	Customer query time Order lead time Frequency of delivery Actual versus theoretical throughput time Cycle time
Dependability	Percentage of orders delivered late Average lateness of orders Proportion of products in stock Mean deviation from promised arrival Schedule adherence
Flexibility	Time needed to develop new products/services Range of products/services Machine changeover time Average batch size Time to increase activity rate Average capacity/maximum capacity Time to change schedules
Cost	Minimum delivery time/average delivery time Variance against budget Utilization of resources Labour productivity Added value Efficiency Cost per operation hour

Table 3.2 *Performance objectives and measures*   Source: *Slack et al.* (2001)

Look at the case study below about DaimlerChrysler for an example of a quality performance measure in action.

DaimlerChrysler suffers quality woes: warranty costs surge as managers cut development times

Frankfurt (FTMW) – DaimlerChrysler is plagued by growing quality problems at its luxury car making unit Mercedes-Benz that cost the group €1.7 billion in warranty payments last year, the Financial Times reported. The stock dropped 1 percent to €56, and was one of the biggest decliners in Germany's benchmark DAX Index on Tuesday. The shares have risen about 25 percent this year. Warranty costs – the charges for repairing vehicles still under guarantee – have tripled in two years, the FT said, citing people familiar with the Stuttgart-based company.

The problems at Mercedes-Benz could not come at a worse time for DaimlerChrysler chief executive Juergen Schrempp, who is grappling with a wide-ranging revamp of the ailing US unit Chrysler and loss-making Japanese affiliate Mitsubishi.

Limo go

The world's fifth-biggest carmaker, whose hulking Mercedes S-Class is the preserve of German executives and politicians alike, is more and more reliant on the luxury unit for profits. Mercedes-Benz passenger cars earned half the company's €5.2 billion of adjusted operating profit last year. DaimlerChrysler declined to comment on the warranty cost figure, saying it was business-sensitive information, the FT said. 'Competition has intensified and there is a general trend to broaden warranty services,' the company told the FT. The newspaper reported that the warranty costs were roughly equal to Mercedes-Benz's development expenditure in 2000.

Quality street

The overall increase in sales of passenger cars and the introduction of the compact A-Class and the M-Class sports utility vehicle in the last two years have contributed to the quality problems, the newspaper said. For every M-Class sold, the German company has to shell out almost €2,500 on average for guarantee services, the Financial Times Deutschland reported. That's a record level for Mercedes-Benz, it said. The tank-like M-Class sells for about €50,000. Managers are under pressure to cut development times and save money in the quality control process, the FT reported. The firm has set up 'quality circles' in all major divisions, such as development and production, to tackle the problem, the paper said.

Source: *Manzaroli* (2001)

DaimlerChrysler took action to correct the problem it had been alerted to by the excessive warranty claims by putting in place quality circles. Had these been part of the planning and control process in the first place, it would probably have been alerted earlier. This is also a good example of the costs and benefits of quality management. Managers were under pressure to cut development times and save money in the quality process. But how much more has it cost the company in the long run by making these savings?

Activity 10
Operations planning and control

Objective

This activity will help you to identify and evaluate performance indicators for your own work area.

Task

1 Using the performance objectives and measures table below, tick the particular performance measures you use in your organisation or work area.

2 Add to the bottom of each list any that you use which are not listed here.

Performance objective	Some typical performance measures (indicators)	
Quality	Number of defects per unit	☐
	Level of customer complaints	☐
	Scrap level	☐
	Warranty claims	☐
	Mean time between failures	☐
	Customer satisfaction score	☐
Speed	Customer query time	☐
	Order lead time	☐
	Frequency of delivery	☐
	Actual versus theoretical throughput time	☐
	Cycle time	☐
Dependability	Percentage of orders delivered late	☐
	Average lateness of orders	☐
	Proportion of products in stock	☐
	Mean deviation from promised arrival	☐
	Schedule adherence	☐

Performance objective	Some typical performance measures (indicators)	
Flexibility	Time needed to develop new products/services	☐
	Range of products/services	☐
	Machine changeover time	☐
	Average batch size	
	Time to increase activity rate	☐
	Average capacity/maximum capacity	☐
	Time to change schedules	☐
Cost	Minimum delivery time/average delivery time	☐
	Variance against budget	☐
	Utilisation of resources	☐
	Labour productivity	☐
	Added value	☐
	Efficiency	☐
	Cost per operation hour	☐

3 Consider one or two of your current performance measures that you do not think work very well. Explain why they don't work well – perhaps they are not a true reflection of performance, are too complex to be useful, need to be combined with other measures, statistics are poorly collated, data technology isn't up to the task, etc.

4 Are there alternative performance indicators, perhaps on the above list that you haven't ticked, which might be more suitable? Name any and explain why they might be more suitable.

Performance measures that do not work very well	More suitable performance indicators

Feedback

Any statistical data on its own can be misleading (hence the well-known saying, 'there are lies, damn lies, and statistics'). For example, customer satisfaction scores may not be a true reflection of customer satisfaction if they are based on a limited number of criteria, small samples or unfocused criteria, such as the number of times people complained in the last month. Moreover, the usefulness of statistics lies in the analysis after they have been gathered. If statistics are gathered for the sake of it, but neither analysis as to why the statistics are as they are, nor what to do about performance follows, data collection is pointless. Performance indicators are just that – indicators – they do not tell you anything useful in themselves. You need to ask whether your performance indicators are useful?

Discuss with your team or colleagues your suggestions for improvements.

To add to this activity, in your list of performance measures, write 'p' or 's' for those measures that are product related and those that are service related. This will help you to differentiate a little more clearly between service and product operations.

Quality control tools and techniques

There are various quality tools and techniques that can facilitate the measurement and control of operations. They are usually, but not exclusively, based on sampling and involve quantitative analysis. The two main ones we consider here are statistical process control (SPC) and acceptance sampling.

Process control issues

A number of questions come to mind when using quantitative measurement tools:

◆ What part of the process should be examined? Before, during or after an operation? In other words, the inputs, the process itself or the outputs? Maybe all three parts need to be measured. Moreover, any operational process usually has different stages to the process itself. For example, making whisky involves soaking the barley, initial fermentation, smoking the barley over a peat fire, mashing it, more fermentation, distillation, maturation and storage. So at what stage of the actual process should quantitative checks be made?

♦ When should the process be examined? For example, whisky needs to be matured over a number of years in oak casks or something similar. How often should sample checks be made?

♦ How many products should be checked? All of them, or just a sample? It would be time-consuming and costly to check all mass-produced consumer items. But, particularly where health and safety considerations are paramount, the more you can check the better, as the following example demonstrates. It is about how using a new 100 per cent screening model for retesting smears for possible cancerous cells produced significantly better detection rates than a random selection process.

A Model for 100% Quality Control Rescreening of Negative Papanicolaou Smears Incorporating the AutoPap 300 QC System
Introduction/Purpose: We have attempted to develop a comprehensive QC [quality control] program which will maximize identification of false negatives (FN) due to detection error and lead to documented reduction of FN rates while minimizing increase in workload and cost.

Materials and Methods: Since March 1997 we have utilized a QC program incorporating the AutoPap 300 QC System for 100% automated QC rescreening. Smears categorized as QC-review (QCRV), process review (PRV), review (RV) or no-review/high-risk clinical features (NRHR) are selected for manual rescreening. We compared the identification of FN smears with that of our previous 10% random selection protocol and monitored the impact of this program on FN rates through cytohistologic correlation studies as well as the extent of increased workload and cost.

Results: We documented an approximate 6-fold increase in identification of significant detection errors and decreases of 52.4% and 88.7% in overall and screening FN rates, respectively. The manual rescreen rate increased from 15.7% to 25.5%. Implementation of this program has resulted in increased cost of $5.00/smear, or $2,900 for each extra LSIL or higher abnormality identified.

Conclusion: Implementation of a 100% QC rescreening program using the AutoPap 300 QC System can be an effective means of identifying detection FNs and decreasing FN rates with a limited increase in laboratory cost and workload.

Source: *Marshall and Bentz* (1998)

- What characteristics of a product should be measured? This is normally divided into **variable** and **attribute** characteristics. Variable characteristics include things like length, weight, time, temperature or pressure which go up or down on a continuous scale – the average or mean is the issue here. Attribute characteristics are those to which you can apply two criteria such as yes/no, right/wrong, works/doesn't work, pass/fail, etc. For example, if someone in the UK has more than 80 milligrams of alcohol in their bloodstream per 100 millilitres of blood, they would fail a driving breath test.

- What techniques should be used? For example, statistical process control (SPC) or acceptance sampling.

Type 1 and type 2 errors

One of the inherent problems with sampling is that the sample may not be a true reflection of product quality. For example, a sample of four barrels of chemical waste may reveal that everything is stable, so you assume the same is true for the rest of the batch and take no action. However, it may be that one of the barrels not sampled has reached high levels of combustibility and explodes in transit, killing a railway worker. This is called a type 2 error because you took no action when you should have done. However, had you decided to check all the barrels on the basis of the sample you found, and found they were all stable, this would have been a type 1 error because you took action when you should not have done.

To summarise, a type 1 error involves making corrections where no corrections are needed; a type 2 error involves not making corrections where they are needed.

Acceptance sampling

Acceptance sampling is carried out before or after the operational process. It usually deals with attribute rather than variable characteristics. Sampling the diameters of nuclear fuel pellets, barrels of chemical waste, raw materials from a supplier or dissatisfied customers in a supermarket are all examples of acceptance sampling.

The usual procedure in acceptance sampling is to take a sample from a batch and then accept or reject the batch depending on whether the sample falls within a predefined range.

Sampling plans

There are other approaches to sampling (known as sampling plans), for example:

◆ Double sampling plans – After the first sample is tested, there are three possibilities:

1 Accept the batch.

2 Reject the batch.

3 No decision.

If no decision is the outcome, a second sample is taken. The results are then combined before a final decision is made.

◆ Multiple sampling plans – an extension of double sampling where more than two samples are needed to reach a conclusion.

◆ Sequential sampling plans – the ultimate extension of multiple sampling where items are selected from a batch one at a time and, after inspection of each item, a decision is made to accept or reject the batch or to select another item.

Look again at the case study on detecting false smear results. You can see that the previous technique used (10 per cent random selection) is an example of acceptance sampling because the test should reveal either cancerous cells or healthy cells. This system involved type 2 errors. The new 100 per cent process control programme produces type 1 errors; quality and defect detection is enhanced, although it involves greater costs, time and work than 10 per cent random selection.

Statistical process control (SPC)

Statistical process control developed in the 1920s in the US and the UK. It focuses on checking an operation during its process by sampling. It can check variable or attribute characteristics. The purpose of the sampling is to detect unacceptable variables or attributes – those that go beyond set ranges or limits – and then to make corrections to the process to reduce or eliminate them.

> **A control chart is a form of traffic signal whose operation is based on evidence from a small number of samples taken at random during a process.**
>
> Oakland **(2003)**

Control charts

SPC uses control charts to document samples over a period of time. Here's a simple example – Figure 3.5 – which can show a variable trend or an attribute trend.

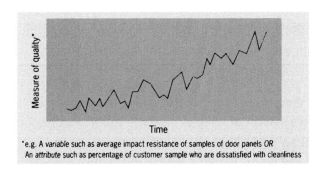

Figure 3.5 *Chart showing trends in variables or attributes*

Source: *Slack et al.* (2001)

Depending on the parameters (or control limits) set, the chart would trigger a warning, action could then be taken to find out the causes of the variations and these could be remedied – see Figure 3.6.

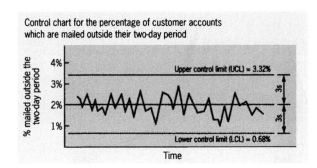

Figure 3.6 *Control limits*   Source: *Slack et al.* (2001)

Activity 11
Six sigma

Objective

Sigma, the symbol for standard deviation, a topic you may vaguely remember from school statistics, has become part of a major business improvement process called 'six sigma'. How has a statistical figure and symbol become the sign of a major business improvement process?

This activity asks you to use the Internet to investigate what six sigma is and how companies are using it.

Task

Six sigma has its roots in statistical process control. It is therefore important to understand some of the terms used. The following terms will be explained:

◆ Normal distribution

◆ Natural variation of the process

◆ Tolerance or specification range

◆ Process capability.

All processes vary in some way or another. If you take several samples from the process, as the number of samples increases you would expect the values (for example, the weight of cornflakes in a box or the number of paperclips in a pack) to show a normal distribution. That is, most values measured will be around the value you are trying to control (the process average/mean), and a tailing off on each side of values that were above or below the average.

Figure 3.7 *Graph showing Normal Distribution*

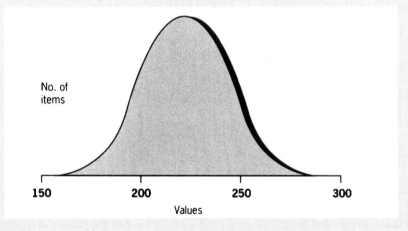

A normal distribution in statistics means that most of the values measured will fall within 3 standard deviations (represented by the symbol sigma Σ) either side of the average value, in fact 99.7 per cent of the values. So in controlling processes it is said that the **natural variation of the process** is described by ±3 standard deviations either side of the process average.

The operations manager has to answer the question, 'Is this variation in the process acceptable?' To answer this, upper limits and lower limits are set for the process. These limits are the acceptable range of values tolerated by the operation, known as the **tolerance range** or the **specification range**.

A simple measure of the capability of the process is to divide the specification range (the allowable variation) by the natural variation of the process (described by ±3 standard deviations of the mean). A **process capability** of 1 means that the specification range is the same as the natural variation of the process. A process capability of less than 1 means the natural variation is bigger than the specification range – you have problems!

Six sigma

The six sigma quality concept starts with the idea that the natural variation of the process (±3 standard deviations) should be half the specification range. In other words, the specification range for any process should be ±6 standard deviations (six sigma).

What are the implications?

A process capability of 1, where the specification for the process is the same as the natural variation, implies a defect rate of 2.7 per 1,000. This is referred to as 'three sigma' quality. 'Six sigma' quality is considerably more ambitious: it implies a defect rate of only 3.4 defects per million.

Case study

Read the following case study.

Jack Welch, General Electric's chairman and chief executive officer, has set a corporate goal of 'becoming, by the year 2000, a six sigma quality company, which means a company that produces virtually defect-free products, services and transactions'. As he outlined in his address to GE's 1996 and 1997 annual meetings: 'Three to four sigma quality is typically 10–15 per cent of revenues. In GE's case, with over $70bn in revenues, that amounts to some $7–10bn annually, mostly scrap, reworking of parts and rectifying mistakes in transactions. So the financial rationale for embarking on this quality journey is clear.

'But beyond the pure financials, there are even more important rewards that will come with dramatically improved quality. Among them, the unlimited growth from selling products and services universally recognised by customers as being on a completely different plane of quality than those of your competitors... Six sigma will be an exciting journey and the most difficult and invigorating stretch goal we have ever undertaken. The magnitude of the challenge of going from 35,000 defects per million to fewer than four defects is huge. It will require us to reduce defect rates 10,000 fold – about 84 per cent for five consecutive years ... [but] we want to make our quality so special, so valuable to our customers, so important to their success that our products and services become their only real value choice.'

Source: *Hill* (2000)

Task

Carry out an Internet investigation to find out the features and benefits of six sigma quality.

You can use a search engine to identify sources, but first have a look at some of the sites highlighted below.

As you gather information about six sigma, use the questions below to help structure your information. Record your findings.

1   Based on the introduction to six sigma given earlier, if three sigma quality is equivalent to a process capability of 1, what is the process capability equivalent to six sigma quality?

2   Why has a technical term buried in statistical techniques become synonymous with major company quality programmes?

3   What are the principles of six sigma?

4   Where did the six sigma initiative start and why?

5   What techniques are used in the approach?

6   How similar are the techniques to the conventional quality tools and techniques referred to in Theme 2: **Improvement tools and techniques**?

7   Why does GE focus not just on the average or mean value of the process, but put particular emphasis on the range of values or variation?

8   Is it worth trying to achieve such high standards of conformance?

9   Taking the progression of quality from inspection to TQM, as highlighted in our first section on the language of quality, can you draw any parallels between specific companies like GE or other businesses on their journey in quality?

10 What are the benefits of six sigma to organisations?

Useful sites to check

Companies that have implemented six sigma – General Electric (GE) and Motorola are two well-known advocates.

GE's website www.ge.com/sixsigma has numerous information sources, in particular its overview of six sigma and references to conference proceedings. The GE home page has a student page where a range of information about the company has been grouped.

Bettermanagement.com This site offers a six sigma resource centre in its library. There are extensive business articles and white papers from practitioners and experts, available free of charge. Select the LIBRARY and 'Browse content'.

The Department of Trade and Industry (DTI) publishes a factsheet on six sigma on its website at www.dti.gov.uk/bestpractice/operations/quality.htm

The Juran Institute at www.juran.com has several articles on six sigma. The site also provides a history of Joseph Juran, who was one of the founding fathers of quality.

Feedback

You can find quite a lot of information about six sigma on the Internet. If you were able to visit some of the sites suggested above, you should have been able to find enough information to answer the questions and build your understanding of the subject.

You may want to discuss the benefits and drawbacks of six sigma with learning colleagues.

◆ Recap

Define operations management and identify five performance measures for quality operations

◆ Operations management is the term used for the management activities and decisions associated with managing the production and delivery of products and services to meet business goals.

◆ The effectiveness of an operation can be measured against five performance objectives: quality, speed, cost, dependability and flexibility.

Explore processes for designing products, services and operational processes that meet business goals

◆ Designing products and services is a transformation process that can be managed in the same way as any other operation. Involving customers and suppliers at the design stage helps to ensure the quality of the final product or service.

◆ Technology, the supply chain, physical layout and the design of people's jobs are all key considerations in designing an operational process.

Identify key activities and issues in planning and control

◆ Planning involves estimating what needs to be done to meet customer demand efficiently and effectively. Control is the process of monitoring, intervention and correction to ensure operations go according to the plan or to cope with changes in the plan.

◆ Push and pull control mechanisms are used to control the volume of material in a manufacturing process. Push control is supply led. Pull control, for example JIT, is demand led and results in less build-up of inventory.

Examine two techniques for the measurement and control of operations

◆ Acceptance sampling involves taking a sample from a batch and then accepting or rejecting the whole batch depending on whether the attribute you are measuring falls within an acceptable range.

◆ Statistical process control involves using control charts to track particular variable and attribute characteristics of a sample of products, over time. This will identify whether or not the process is operating within set parameters.

◆ Where measurement techniques indicate a problem with the process, managers will need to ascertain causes and take remedial action.

▶▶ More @

Brown, S., Blackmon, K., Cousins, P, and Maylor, H. (2001) *Operations Management,* **Butterworth-Heinemann**
This comprehensive text provides cutting-edge input into operations management theory and practice and has sections dedicated to performance management and improvement.

Slack, N., Chambers, S. and Johnson, R. (2001) 3rd edition, *Operations Management,* **FT Prentice Hall**
This comprehensive book has its own dedicated website for additional resources – www.booksites.net/slack.

Brown, S., Lamming, R., Bessar, J. and Jones, P. (2000) *Strategic operations management,* **Butterworth-Heinemann**
This book combines four themes to shed new light on the strategic importance of operations: strategy, services, innovation and management of relationships, both in the supply chain and with other stakeholders.

http://iomnet.org.uk/index.htm
The Institute of Operations Management is a professional body for persons involved in production management, supply chain management and operations management in manufacturing and service industries.

4 Techniques for planning and control

Developing the operation so that it is able to satisfy fluctuating levels of demand, without compromising quality levels, is a fundamental aspect of operations management. This theme looks in more detail at three ways in which organisations seek to do this:

♦ planning and controlling the capacity of the operation

♦ planning and controlling inventory so that stock is always available to meet demand

♦ managing the supply chain, starting with the flow of goods, services and information starting from suppliers and ending with finished products for customers and end users.

You will:

♦ **Explore how to carry out capacity planning and control successfully**

♦ **Consider the key issues in inventory planning and control**

♦ **Consider JIT and MRP as holistic approaches to inventory planning and control**

♦ **Learn about supply chain management and its key components.**

Capacity planning and control

Capacity planning and control is about the organisation's ability to supply the necessary goods and services to meet the demands of its customers. It is about how to ensure employees, inventory, equipment, processing and scheduling is organised to meet different levels of demand, that is, **fluctuations** in demand.

Fluctuations in demand are inevitable for any organisation due to daily, weekly, seasonal, micro and macro-economic factors.

Why is it important?

There are a number of good reasons for capacity planning and control:

♦ Costs – too much capacity may increase costs, for example, by having to pay for labour and inventory, or the fixed costs on products which cannot be sold.

♦ Income – too little capacity means that you are not selling as much as you could, for example, a pub which only has a couple of servers on a busy Saturday night may lose customers and income to other pubs.

♦ Quality – for example, computer suppliers which have inadequate numbers of customer-service staff will lose quality in their operations (as measured, for example, in terms of time required to answer customer calls and deal with customer problems). Manufacturers which have insufficient machines to complete orders in time will not be satisfying customer expectations (quality was defined in Theme 1 as 'consistent conformance to customers' expectations').

The Internet has come under considerable criticism for its inability to cope with the amount of traffic it receives. This has resulted in slow upload/download speeds, unreliable connections and the inability to relay high-quality video and audio content. Faster technologies based on broadbanding and digital technologies which offer higher capacity data transmission are an attempt to solve this problem.

Capacity constraints

There are some **long-term constraints** on any organisation as regards capacity. For example, if you build a concert hall or football stadium, your capacity is limited to the number of seats you can safely install. A manufacturer is limited by the capacity of its process technology; a retailer by the size of its store.

However, capacity planning and control in the sense meant here is more about **medium to short-term capacity**, and capacity that can be manipulated. For example, a football stadium or concert hall will have events for which it is not full to capacity, so the number of employees and the size of the services it needs should take this into account.

Stages in capacity planning and control

There are three key stages to capacity planning and control:

1 Forecast the demand levels.

2 Choose an appropriate capacity plan.

3 Control capacity through monitoring and review.

Forecasting

Tool predicts network capacity

Clairvoyant Software Inc. has developed a new capacity planning tool that predicts for network and systems managers when they will need to add more bandwidth or computing resources to support the growth of Internet traffic. The Saratoga, Calif., company's new Forecast Resource Manager is designed to predict when network or system resources will reach saturation, allowing operators to stay ahead of demand. The Linux-based tool comes in an Internet Access version and an e-Commerce version.

The Internet Access version, which began shipping last week, can predict capacity requirements for dial-up and dedicated Internet access, VPNs (virtual private networks), and dedicated WAN links that deliver IP services. It gathers and presents usage data by resource type, such as point-of-presence location, VPN or uplink vendor.

The e-Commerce version, due at the end of next month, can predict capacity requirements by allowing users to specify saturation levels of CPUs, memory or disk storage for Web, application or database servers. The tool then monitors those resources for usage trends. It also predicts when WAN links or Ethernet switch ports will reach saturation.

Source: *PC Week* (2000)

Forecasting future demand is no easy matter. It involves looking at both historical data and future events. It could involve using marketing analysis, industry analysis, PESTLE analysis or a specialist capacity planning tool (as in the case study above). It's easy enough, say, for a retailer to look back and predict that levels of demand will pick up (peak) in certain periods, for example Christmas and bank holidays, but more difficult to predict how successful it will be in selling its products on these occasions.

The foot-and-mouth outbreak in the UK in the spring of 2001 left many service providers in the countryside in a difficult economic condition. While they were gearing up for the beginning of the season, the prohibitions on moving through the countryside meant they had few or no customers. How could they possibly have anticipated this macro event when planning their forward capacity requirements?

Choosing a capacity plan

There are three typical capacity plans an organisation can adopt to cope with forecast fluctuations in demand:

♦ level capacity plan

♦ chase demand plan

♦ manage demand plan.

Level capacity plan

In a level capacity plan, capacity levels are maintained at a constant rate regardless of the fluctuations in demand – the same number of employees, machines, level of processing, etc. This is suitable for organisations where demand is relatively stable and/or inventory can be kept at reasonable cost. The inventory will build up during times of low demand to be available when it's needed in periods of high demand, so the capacity balances out over time.

This plan is not suitable for organisations which produce fashionable or perishable products or high-tech products which quickly become obsolete. It isn't suitable for organisations which have huge swings in seasonal demand, such as holiday hotels, though a central London hotel could use a level capacity plan as it is likely to have a fairly consistent level of demand. Public sector organisations, such as the civil service, local government, teaching or nursing, often run on a level capacity basis.

Chase demand plan

In a chase demand plan, the capacity 'chases' the demand, so the capacity is made as flexible as possible to meet varying levels of demand. This is more typical of modern approaches to capacity planning and inventory control such as just-in-time.

It is particularly suitable for seasonal-based service organisations and organisations with sudden variations in demand such as supermarkets, hotels and restaurants. It works well where there are flexible working arrangement such as part-time, temporary, annualised hours, contract and overtime arrangements. It works less well where employment regulation results in high costs for hiring and firing employees.

Manage demand plan

In a manage demand plan, the organisation tries to match the demand more equally to the capacity by transferring the demand from peak to quiet periods, thereby smoothing out the fluctuations. For example, a typical supply and demand tactic is to lower prices when there is little demand and put them up when there is high demand to encourage customers to buy in the quiet periods. Examples of this tactic include low-cost, off-peak holidays and hotel breaks and 'happy hours' in pubs.

It should be noted that many organisations actually use a mixture of these plans because they are required to reduce costs and inventory, minimise capital investment and provide a responsive and customer-oriented approach simultaneously.

Controlling capacity

Controlling capacity is about gathering data on capacity levels on a regular basis. This may include monitoring inventory, idle processes, productivity and units sold for the period to compare actual capacity with forecast levels. A specialist monitoring tool may be used such as the Forecast Resource Manager (see the case study above) which, as well as forecasting, 'gathers and presents usage data by resource type' and 'monitors ... for usage trends'.

Plans then have to be adjusted as necessary for the next period, and the planning and control process starts again.

Activity 12
Capacity planning and control

Objective

Use this activity to assess the capacity needs of your own work area.

Task

1 Assess the capacity needs of your own work area based on the following criteria:

   ♦ Number of employees and their working arrangements (work organisation) – are there sufficient employees or too many? Are they at work when work needs to be done, or not?

   ♦ Inventory requirements – space to place stock or deal with customers, for example, any queues?

   ♦ Processing – efficiency or productivity of your work area in terms of things like the capacity limits of equipment, layout and job skills.

2 Complete the table with your assessments and recommendations for improvements.

Number of employees and their working arrangements

Analysis of current situation:	Recommendations for improvements:

Inventory requirements

Analysis of current situation:	Recommendations for improvements:

Processing

Analysis of current situation:	Recommendations for improvements:

Feedback

If this exercise is worth doing, any recommendations you have come up with should be worth carrying forward. After further analysis, discuss these with your manager.

Inventory planning and control

Inventory, or stock – for the purposes of inventory planning and control – is **the accumulation of material inputs and outputs in a transformation system**. Inventory can be raw materials, part-finished or finished products. For example, a car manufacturer has an inventory of car components, machines, chemicals, etc. (inputs) as well as an inventory of half-finished cars waiting on assembly lines for the next part of the transformation process (part-outputs) and finished cars waiting in car lots to be sold to dealers (outputs). The word is used in all contexts. In the micro or macro-economic context, you may hear that inventory levels are up. This refers to outputs and is usually a bad sign as it means goods are not being sold.

> **Inventory control is the activity which organises the availability of its items to the customers.**
>
> **Wild
> (2002)**

Inventory planning and control is about ensuring that stock is at the right level to ensure **supply meets demand**. We mentioned a similar aim when talking about capacity planning. However, there we were considering resources in general, not just material resources, and were less focused on outputs as a stock factor.

Why is there a need for inventory planning and control?

The first need arises because of fluctuations in demand. If there is a sudden surge in demand and you have no inventory, you will not be able to keep up with this demand. Conversely, if there is a drop in demand, you may have more inventory than you can effectively store. In both cases, you are losing revenue because you are either not selling as much as you could or not selling as much as you thought you could.

The second need arises out of the first. Inventory is a cost issue. The following costs are relevant in this regard:

♦ Storage costs – it costs money to store goods, money for lighting, energy, equipment, employees, space and rent (if applicable). The more inventory you have, the more it costs.

◆ Obsolescence costs – most stored goods have a shelf-life. If they are stored too long, they may perish (for example food products) or go out of date (for example fashion items).

◆ Capital costs – these arise because of the lag between buying supplies and selling products. The longer the gap, the more you are living on savings or borrowings.

So, inventory planning and control can improve your revenue and reduce your costs. Organisations need some inventory as a **buffer**, or safety valve, against sudden surges in demand, but too much can be costly. Judging this fine line is the key to good inventory planning and control.

How much to order and when to order

The crucial planning decision for the stock purchaser is how much to order and when to order – the **volume–timing continuum**. Order too much and you face inventory costs if you cannot sell. On the other hand, you may get a price discount from the supplier if you order in bulk. Order too little and you lose your price discount and may not have enough supplies to meet demand. Order too early, and you may have too much inventory for a short period. Order too late and you run out of supplies for a short period.

There are a number of approaches to the volume-timing decision such as:

◆ order the same amount on a regular basis

◆ order the same amount on a irregular basis

◆ order different amounts on a regular basis

◆ order different amounts on an irregular basis.

There are advantages and disadvantages to each, but the sophistication of planning and control increases as you go down the list. For example, ordering the same amount on a regular basis is an easy system to implement, but there is a danger of unnecessary, wasteful inventory; ordering different amounts on an irregular basis involves continuous forecasting, detailed organisation and a sophisticated supplier information network, but the potential advantages are an inventory which closely matches supply and demand and eliminates wastage.

Another factor in the volume-timing decision is to balance the costs of holding inventory (storage, obsolescence and capital) against the costs of making an order (price discounts and delivery costs). There are various mathematical models which attempt to do this, such as the economic order quantity (EOQ) formula and the economic batch quantity (EBQ) model.

> Generally, the more you buy, the more your holding costs and the less your order costs – and vice versa.

Inventory analysis and control systems

Classification and measurement

Any inventory analysis and control system requires a classification and measurement system. Classification should not be just by number, product type, etc.; it should also prioritise stock on a **value** basis. For example, running out of one component may be more serious than running out of another because it is more essential to the running of the production line. Other items may be used more frequently than others and they are generally classified by **usage value** (rate of use multiplied by monetary value).

> In a typical inventory, 80 per cent of usage value is accounted for by only 20 per cent of stock types – an application of Pareto's law. This has led to a classification system known as ABC: class A has highest usage value and lowest number of stock types, class B has medium usage value and a higher number of stock types, class C has lowest usage value and the highest number of stock types. This allows the most important stock items to be closely controlled.

Measurement systems for inventory include **inventory value** (worth of stock at any one time) and **stock turn** (rate of stock turnover).

Inventory information systems

The necessity for more sophisticated approaches to inventory planning and control has resulted in the growth of complex information systems which can measure inventory levels and reorder stock automatically.

> Tesco uses an extranet network called the Tesco Information Exchange (TIE) for, among other things, automatic stock reordering. Whenever a sale is made at the till via electronic point of sale (EPOS), an order for stock replenishment of the item is automatically generated.

Inventory analysis and control systems typically update stock records and generate regular reports on stock position to enable managers to monitor actual inventory against forecasts.

These systems may also be able to readjust forecasts as necessary.

Just-in-time (JIT)

JIT is not just an inventory planning and control system. It is a sophisticated development of inventory planning and control to include not only materials requirements but also resources, both physical and human.

It is a holistic, quality-based approach to requirements planning and control which uses information systems, quality tools and techniques, capacity scheduling, continuous improvement and employee involvement to meet demand instantly (just in time) with perfect quality and no waste.

It is a pull system as opposed to a push system.

JIT aims not only to meet the exact demands of customers when they order, its production process is also tuned into demand so that it won't produce what isn't needed. In this way inventory is – in terms of volume and time – kept to an absolute minimum. Just-in-time is the original lean-and-mean system.

JIT uses a system called *kanban* to control inventory. *Kanban* is the Japanese word for card or signal and is the trigger for moving resources in and through the organisation. *Kanban* is a visible card, which can be electronic.

For example, Ford uses a real-time, wireless, parts replenishment system developed with WhereNet in some of its assembly plants. Based on tags attached to the supplies, fixed-position readers and browser-enabled software, it allows production workers to get parts delivered to their workstations by electronic call as and when they need them.

Constant tracking of the parts by the information system ensures more productive management of the call system. It has brought about time and cost savings through reduced maintenance and increased efficiency.

JIT sees inventory as a 'blanket of obscurity' which lies over the production system and prevents problems being noticed.

Source: *Slack et al.* (2001)

Slack et al. use an interesting metaphor to illustrate this – a ship in water – see Figure 4.1.

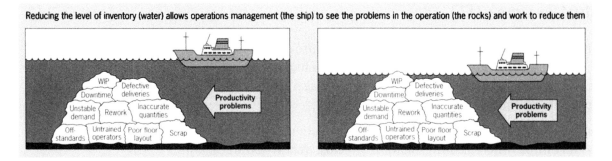

Figure 4.1 *JIT uncovers problems*   Source: *Slack et al.* (2001)

One of the problems with such a refined approach to inventory is that sudden and unexpected events can disrupt the process. For example, the UK petrol crisis in September 2000, when lorry drivers blocked depots in protest against high fuel charges, disrupted just-in-time and *kanban* manufacturing processes as inventories were too low to cover the lack of supplier deliveries.

MRP

Another holistic and sophisticated approach to inventory planning and control is a push-based system called MRP. This arose in the 1970s and originally meant 'materials requirements planning' (MRP I). A new variation arose in the 1980s –'manufacturing resources planning' (MRP II). It is a complex, computer-based system which relates inventory and material or resource requirements to customer orders, forecast demand and a master production schedule – see Figure 4.2. In some of its guises, it includes capacity planning and, as MRP II, links all the resources of a company to financial and accounting systems.

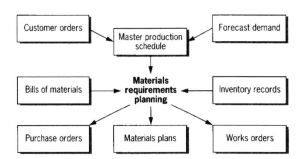

Figure 4.2 *Materials requirements planning (MRP I) schematic*

Source: *Slack et al.* (2001)

ERP

ERP, or enterprise resource planning, arose in the 1990s and is a further development of MRP. ERP is the ultimate integrated resources system. It links all the computer systems into one integrated database to reflect the planning and control systems of the whole organisation – see Figure 4.3.

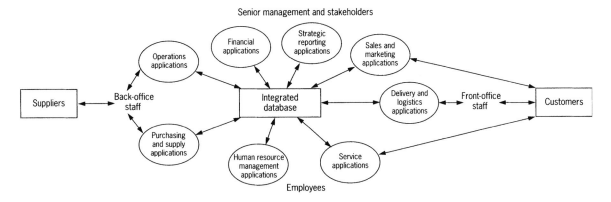

Figure 4.3 *ERP*   Source: *Slack et al.* (2001)

The implications of planning and control in one area can, therefore, be reflected in another area. These include financial, people, sales and operations implications. SAP, Oracle, Baan and PeopleSoft are some of the software companies involved in this area.

The enormity of the task of implementing an ERP system has already got the critics working. Companies have spent millions trying to implement ERP only to find it doesn't work properly or is out of date as soon as it is implemented because it takes so long *to* implement. Dow Chemical spent $500 million on its system, which took seven years to implement and was out of date as soon as it was implemented.

Activity 13
Inventory issues

Objective

Use this activity to identify inventory problems and determine solutions.

Task

1 Consider the problems faced by companies during holiday periods as you read the case study below.

Case study

E-Commerce Firms Grapple With Inventory Issues

Susan Daniher spent last year's holiday shopping season frantically packing DVDs into boxes with all the other company executives from DVDExpress.com, just to meet the unexpectedly high demand. This time around, company officials are hoping to be better prepared, although Daniher, the company's vice president of marketing, acknowledged that 'holiday shopping online is like the wild west. You can never tell how many people are going to shop.'

For experienced e-commerce sites as well as the many newcomers, the holiday guessing game is in full swing. What's going to be the top seller? How many people are needed to get merchandise out the door? Will the company's executives be spending their Christmas Eve packing $59.95 crème brûlée-making kits (complete with blowtorch) instead of wrapping presents with their families? 'If we had a Magic 8 ball, we'd be perfect,' said Tracy Randall, chief operating officer of Santa Monica-based Cooking.com. 'This isn't a science, it's an art.' For many Web sites, it's an art that must be refined in the coming years. Americans are projected to spend $6 billion shopping online during the 1999 holiday season, according to Jupiter Communications, compared with $3.2 billion a year ago. By 2003, U.S. consumers could be spending more than $70 billion online during the holidays. But in the Internet world, 2003 is a long time off, and the lessons learned by Christmases past are tentatively being put into effect this year.

To a certain extent, Randall said, Cooking.com can predict what customers will order. Most Web shoppers will buy the items that are heavily promoted, such as gift baskets and items that have been reduced. 'I think during the holidays most people feel like, "Tell me what to buy,"' she said. With that in mind, Cooking.com has upped its inventory at a warehouse in Ontario, with items like the Whirley Pop Popcorn Popper and the aforementioned crème brûlée-making kit. 'We offer them a degree of flexibility,' said California distribution president Larry Willett. 'Our job is to give them rubber walls.'

Willett said e-commerce companies electronically transmit the orders as they come through on their Web sites. Workers at the warehouse then 'pick and pack' – and occasionally even gift wrap – the item and send it on its way. At that point, the warehouse sends a confirmation back to the company with a tracking number that can be passed along to customers. For the holiday rush, California Distribution hired an additional 25 people to speed up the shipping process.

eHobbies launched in October, but chief executive Brad Sobel said the Web site has been planning for the holiday rush since it was funded by eCompanies earlier this year. 'We've aimed our inventory at the holiday season,' Sobel said. 'We have depth in all the right places, because if folks come here and you're out of stock, then you're out of business.' Sobel said company officials were able to set their inventory based on traditional holiday buying patterns for hobby aficionados – train sets, for example, are a huge holiday item but not very big the rest of the year.

Other first-year e-commerce sites can base their inventories on the experiences of their brick-and-mortar stores. Petsmart.com, the Pasadena-based online division of the pet supplies retailer, shares warehouses in Anaheim and New York with its real-world counterpart. 'One of the benefits is that Petsmart has had experience with the holiday season for 12 years,' said chief executive Tom McGovern. 'They already know that 80 per cent of the dog owners and 70 per cent of the cat owners do buy Christmas presents for their pets.' This year, Petsmart has loaded up with pet treats – and edible Christmas cards, because 'dogs can't read,' McGovern said.

As for DVDExpress.com, it has a new warehouse with more than five times the space it had last year. Fifty new employees were hired for the holidays and an automatic re-order system was put in place to monitor inventory and re-order when supplies run low. But even with the new warehouse, extra help and pumped-up inventories, Daniher still has a pretty good idea of where she will be during the holiday season: at work, in the warehouse, frantically packing DVDs.

Source: *Donahue* (1999)

2 What problems do companies face during holiday periods which have implications for inventory?

Holiday period problems:

3 What solutions are used to control inventory and ensure supply matches demand?

Supply and demand solutions:

4 Think about any problems you have in your work area that have implications for inventory. What action can you take?

Actions to counter problems:

Feedback

2 These kinds of problems could occur during holiday periods and have implications for inventory:

◆ It's difficult to predict how many people will shop

◆ It's difficult to predict what people will want to buy

◆ It's difficult to know how many employees to hire.

3 You may have noted some of these solutions:

◆ promoting items to make predictions easier (managing demand)

◆ basing predictions on previous years and previous experiences

◆ basing predictions on 'traditional holiday buying patterns for hobby aficionados'

◆ hiring more staff

◆ using technology, for example an automatic re-order system

◆ creating more inventory capacity

◆ building up inventory.

4 You may want to discuss your ideas with an interested colleague or your manager.

Supply chain management

Supply chain management is the management of the flow of inputs and outputs from suppliers to customers – see Figure 4.4. This includes the flow of people, materials and data/information.

Figure 4.4 *The organisation as a supply chain*

Its key components include:

♦ procurement (purchasing supplies)

♦ order processing

♦ production scheduling

♦ inventory control

♦ transportation and warehousing

♦ customer service and relationship management.

Supply chain management is a pull system like JIT, which means each part of the supply chain responds only when triggered (pulled) by a preceding part. In other words, it responds to customer **demand**, as opposed to a push system which is **supply** led. MRP is essentially a push system because everything is controlled (pushed) by the master production schedule.

An important consideration of supply chain management is adding value to each step of the chain so that both the organisation and the customer get best value from the product – in other words, costs and prices down, quality up.

Value is an important concept in providing quality.

Procter and Gamble uses a programme called Streamline Logistics II to reduce unloading time in food retailer warehouses. By combining activity-based costing and electronic data interchange (EDI) with drop-and-hook programmes and elimination of pallet exchanges, the company expects to remove non-value-added costs and improve consumer value – saving $50 million to pass on to customers.

Now consider some key planning and control ideas for supply chain management which focus on its key components.

Purchasing

Purchasing, or procurement, is about buying goods from suppliers as inputs to your transformation process. The way this is carried out has changed considerably since the arrival of Internet technology and e-commerce solutions. Notably, purchasing can be carried out through specially developed extranets. More recently, e-marketplaces and exchanges have been set up where suppliers compete for contracts using e-procurement software. One such is Covisint, a global, e-business exchange for the automotive industry – www.covisint.com. Not all e-procurement ventures have been successful, as is the case with other first-wave Internet ideas, but as with any new technology, people will learn how best to use it through experimentation, evaluation and adaptation.

Whatever the procurement system, performance needs to be measured against the usual objectives of quality, speed, dependability, flexibility and cost. For example, some suppliers use supplier quality assurance (SQA) programmes to improve their systems, equipment, procedures and training. These programmes may then link into ISO 9000 quality standards.

Distribution

If purchasing is the first stage in the supply chain, distribution may be considered the last. Distribution is concerned with delivering the products from the manufacturer to the customer. This involves other supply chain processes such as warehousing, inventory control and transportation. Computerisation has also made a difference to this part of supply chain planning and control.

Intermec Introduces Comprehensive Mobile Computing System for Logistics Industry
EVERETT, WASHINGTON STATE, USA – i-gistics™, a complete mobile hardware and software solution designed to enable delivery fleets to automate their logistics operations, is now available from Intermec Technologies Corp. i-gistics™ provides proof of delivery and more to automate the entire pick-up and delivery process. Drivers using i-gistics™ Mobile Delivery software are able to update shipment status, electronically process deliveries, pick-ups and returns as well as capture signatures for proof of delivery. These features help companies minimize paperwork, reduce lost shipments, increase information accuracy and avoid delivery disputes...

According to a recent report issued by the DOT [Department of Transport], 'The Changing Face of Transportation', truck ton-miles are expected to grow by 88% by the year 2025. The trend will be towards 'smaller, more frequent shipments and demands for increased reliability... carriers face constant pressure to reduce operating costs.' The i-gistics™ solution enables private fleets, LTL carriers and third-party logistics companies to meet these demands by providing real-time data transmission between drivers, dispatchers and distribution centers, ensuring cost-effective, timely and reliable shipments that can be tracked door-to-door.

Source: *Business Wire* (2001a)

Note how the case study stresses the importance of cost, speed ('timely') and dependability ('reliability').

Network relationships

Close co-operation between suppliers, producers and distributors is an important aspect of supply chain management. The closer everybody in the supply chain can work together, the more synchronised the operation can become, eliminating system lags and bringing down costs. For example, one approach to inventory forecasting and replenishment is called jointly managed inventory (JMI). Typically, teams of buyers/sellers such as distributors and manufacturers collaborate on synchronising and integrating their planning and control processes at an operations level.

JMI is a refinement of a process called vendor managed inventory (VMI) where the seller manages the buyer's inventory and is responsible for issuing purchase orders, for example, where a wholesaler controls a retailer's inventory. These processes rely on integrated information systems based on EDI (electronic data interchange) and PoS (point of sale) for control of the operation. Performance measures for this process could be based on inventory value, stock turn, fill rate (percentage of order completed), number of purchase orders per month, total transportation costs, stock returns.

Activity 14
The supply chain

Objective

Use this activity to define and also to evaluate your supply chain network.

In this task, you will identify the supply chain network of your work area or organisation, then evaluate it.

Task

1 Using arrows and boxes, draw your supply chain network with yourself in the centre as 'processor'. Make sure you include both internal and external customers and suppliers.

Your supply chain network:

2 Indicate what you do as the processor and what the customers and suppliers do.

What your suppliers do:

What you do as processor: *What your customers do:*

3 Make some notes of any supply chain problems you have –
purchasing, inventory, distribution, network relationships – and how
you think they could be solved, for example technology, new work
arrangements, SLAs, outsourcing, tendering, inventory controls,
quality systems, etc.

Problems with supply chain	How to resolve problems

Feedback

Discuss your design and supply chain network solutions with
your colleagues to see what they think.

◆ Recap

Explore how to carry out capacity planning and control successfully

- There are three approaches to managing capacity
  - Do not change output to meet demand – level demand plan
  - Change output so that it matches demand (for example JIT)
  - Try to influence demand so that it matches capacity (for example through pricing).

Consider the key issues in inventory planning and control

- When planning how much inventory to hold, organisations need to balance the requirement to be able to meet demand with the costs of storage, obsolescence and capital associated with holding inventory.

- For control purposes, inventory should be classified by usage value as well as volume. The ABC system prioritises controlling the most important stock items by classifying stocks as type A, B or C according to usage value.

Consider JIT and MRP as holistic approaches to inventory planning and control

- MRP – materials requirement planning – is a push system that calculates the materials requirements and creates the necessary production plans to satisfy known and forecast orders.

- JIT – Just-in-Time – is a pull system which minimises inventory by trying to meet actual demand instantly with perfect quality, fast throughput and no waste.

Learn about supply chain management and its key components

- Close co-operation and sharing of information between suppliers, producers and distributors in the supply chain is essential for building understanding. Each step in the chain must add value, keeping costs and prices down and quality up.

- Purchasing and distribution are both key components of an efficient and responsive supply chain.

▶▶ **More @**

Brown, S., Blackmon, K., Cousins, P, and Maylor, H. (2001)
Operations Management, **Butterworth-Heinemann**
This comprehensive text provides cutting-edge input into operations
management theory and practice and has sections dedicated to
performance management and improvement.

Slack, N., Chambers, S. and Johnson, R. (2001), 3rd edition,
Operations Management, **FT Prentice Hall**
This comprehensive book has its own dedicated website for
additional resources – www.booksites.net/slack.

Brown, S., Lamming, R., Bessar, J. and Jones, P. (2000) *Strategic*
operations management, **Butterworth-Heinemann**
This book combines four themes to shed new light on the strategic
importance of operations: strategy, services, innovation and
management of relationships, both in the supply chain and with
other stakeholders.

The **DTI** offers a free toolkit for supply chain management with
guides, case studies and further information links at
www.dti.gov.uk/bestpractice/operations/supply.htm and another on
online purchasing at www.dti.gov.uk/bestpractice/operations/
purchasing.htm

Wild, T. (2002) *Best Practice in Inventory Management*, **Elsevier**
Butterworth-Heinemann
This book focuses on helping companies improve the management
of inventories.

Quality in health, safety and environment

So far in this book, we have focused on quality from the perspective of the customer and on how operations management techniques can help organisations to deliver quality products and services.

> **Health and safety and quality are two sides of the same coin.**
>
> **Health and Safety Executive (1993)**

There is an ever-growing awareness in organisations that quality management is broader than this and also involves being health and safety conscious and environmentally friendly. This brief section looks at the application of quality concepts to health, safety and the environment and signposts you to sources of further information.

You will:

♦ **Assess how a quality approach can improve health, safety and environmental practices**

♦ **Identify ways of improving your health, safety and environmental culture.**

Health, safety and the environment

Health and safety

The **Good Neighbour Scheme** invites you to share your health and safety expertise. Your contractors and suppliers, neighbouring firms and local schools could benefit from your knowledge and skills. The Scheme is about playing your part in the supply chain, and the local community.

But it also makes sound business sense. You probably work with others, as a client, contractor, subcontractor or supplier. Health and safety management is integral to the successful completion of a contract, or to the delivery of goods on time and to the required quality standards. One accident with one employer will have knock-on effects on others in the chain by disrupting supply or services.

Source: *Health and Safety Executive* (www)

You can't say you are producing quality goods if they contain harmful chemicals and are so designed that people could easily be injured. As the case study asserts, poor health and safety practice could disrupt your supply chain, affect delivery, have implications for your contract and drive down your quality standards.

Health and safety in the UK is surrounded by standards (OHS, BS and EN) which build on, or integrate with, quality standards such as ISO 9000. You may use quality standards to demonstrate compliance with health and safety legislation. For example, you may demonstrate compliance with the ATEX Directive 1994 on the use of electrical and mechanical equipment and protective systems in potentially explosive atmospheres by adopting ISO 9000 series standards covering manufacturing process control, testing and examination of products and equipment, installation and maintenance, recording and monitoring.

A systems approach to health and safety is not new. Safe systems of work, which require careful instructions and documentation, have been around for some time in the UK. Documentation is of course typical of a quality approach. Read the case study below regarding the BNFL nuclear plant for an example of what happens when systems are not followed.

BNFL nuclear plant
On 20 August 1999, a member of the MOX Demonstration Facility Quality Control Team at the BNFL nuclear plant in Sellafield identified similarities between the secondary pellet diameter data for successive batches of MOX fuel pellets destined for a Japanese client. (As a confirmatory check on diameter, and in accordance with the one per cent acceptable quality level criterion set out in British Standard BS 6001, a sample of 200 pellets which have passed through two previous checking stages is measured a second time.) After further investigation, it appeared that spreadsheet data from the first measurement had been copied over to the spreadsheet for the second measurement check.

The plant was immediately shut down by the Health and Safety Executive's (HSE) Nuclear Inspection Inspectorate (NII). In their subsequent report, 'An investigation into the falsification of pellet diameter data in the MOX Demonstration Facility at the BNFL Sellafield site and the effect of this on the safety of MOX fuel in use', the NII blamed a systematic management failure which allowed various individuals to falsify quality assurance records for fuel pellet diameter measurements. Lack of supervision, poor training, a lack of job redesign (job was tedious), and lack of awareness of the significance of their job were key ingredients in the management failure.

Source: *adapted from Health and Safety Executive (2000)*

A systems approach to health and safety should involve policymaking, organising, planning and implementing, measuring performance, reviewing and auditing. Its key ingredients are the following (all documented):

♦ objectives and standards

♦ policies and procedures

♦ instruction, information and training

♦ communications systems

♦ safe systems of work

♦ monitoring systems

♦ risk assessment

♦ promotion of a health and safety culture.

Environmental standards

By comparison with health and safety standards, environmental standards are relatively new. The ISO 14000 series is now the accepted international standard.

The ISO 14000 series covers the following areas:

♦ environmental management systems – 14001, 14002, 14004

♦ environmental auditing – 14010–12

♦ environmental labels and declarations – 14020–25

♦ environmental performance evaluation – 14031

♦ life cycle assessment – 14040–43.

According to ISO 14000, an environmental management system (EMS) contains the following key elements:

♦ an environmental policy – where the organisation states its intentions and commitment to environmental performance

♦ planning – where the organisation analyses the environmental impact of its operations

♦ implementation and operation – developing and putting into practice processes that will bring about environmental goals and objectives, including support processes such as T&D

♦ checking and corrective action – monitoring and measurement of environmental indicators to ensure that goals and objectives are being met

♦ management review – review of the EMS by the organisation's top management to ensure its continuing suitability, adequacy and effectiveness

♦ continual improvement.

The benefits of an EMS include:

♦ assuring stakeholders of the organisation's commitment to the environment

♦ improved public image

♦ improved cost control/reduced wastage

♦ demonstration of duty of care in line with the Environmental Protection Act 1990

♦ reduced taxation levels through more efficient waste control, for example landfill tax or energy tax

♦ improved processes through use of technologically advanced environmental systems, for example energy efficient lighting or natural gas.

Here is an example of an EMS and health and safety management system rolled into one. As you read it, check to see how far Bristol-Myers Squibb demonstrates compliance with all the elements of an EMS as defined by ISO 14000.

Management Systems: EHS Management System
Bristol-Myers Squibb is a worldwide health and personal care company whose principal businesses are medicines, beauty care, nutritionals and medical devices. It has an environmental and health and safety management system called EHS (environmental, health and safety) with the following ingredients:

♦ Bristol-Myers Squibb Pledge and EHS Policy

♦ EHS Codes of Practice – build upon the 16 principles of the ICC Business Charter for Sustainable Development and the company's EHS Policy (includes a Code of Practice on programmes and procedures – including goals – and one on continual improvement)

♦ EHS Guidance – provides employees with information to support compliance with the Codes of Practice

♦ Employee training and awareness – to ensure that technical and non-technical staff understand their EHS responsibilities and requirements

♦ Management System Self-Assessment – to measure each division's status with regard to implementing the 16 Codes of Practice

♦ Corporate evaluation programme – to evaluate manufacturing, research and development, and distribution facilities worldwide every 24 to 48 months, based on the site's EHS risk profile

♦ Operating Results Database – to track EHS performance in terms of air, water, and land releases, safety statistics and resource consumption

♦ Feedback mechanisms for internal and external stakeholders – to communicate with management and identify opportunities to improve the management system.

Source: *adapted from Bristol-Myers Squibb* (www)

The importance of quality standards in health, safety and the environment is growing as more and more organisations take up the challenge of developing a more sustainable, 21st-century capitalism. They did it before with grim and grimy 19th-century industrial capitalism, so why not again?

Activity 15
Quality in health, safety and the environment

Objectives

Use this activity to:

♦ identify ways of improving your health, safety and environmental culture

♦ explain how a quality approach can improve health and safety practices.

Task: Part 1

Having an effective health, safety and environmental culture is one of the hallmarks of a quality approach in this area. But how can this be instilled? What activities should management carry out?

Make a list on the opposite page of how management can instil an effective health, safety and environmental culture in the organisation – for example, by including health, safety and the environment in its performance standards.

Goals for achieving an effective health, safety and environmental culture:

Task: Part 2

1   Read the following case study.

The Safety Zone

Food safety is one of the most vitally important issues facing the food-service industry. Past outbreaks have demonstrated the devastation and havoc that food-borne illnesses can wreak. They also showed how committed operators and manufacturers are fighting it head-on and with full force.

There have been remarkable advances, both in the technology of food safety and the determination of the industry to assure patrons that the quality and safety of food handling is fully up to par. Investing in certain pieces of equipment will help operators ensure food safety. A wide variety of quick chillers, food temperature probes, gloves and soaps are all worth researching. Properly sanitizing kitchen features such as equipment, utensils and cutting boards will lessen the chances of bacterial growth. Many companies also offer color coding of products, making it easier for employees to use only one color of items for raw meats and another color for vegetables to help eliminate chances of food-borne illnesses.

Prevention, through training and education is essential when it comes to food safety. Operators must be able to not only solve food safety problems, but take measures to stop problems before they happen. Educational seminars offer up-to-date information about issues that operators may not even have considered. Seminars and safety kits also help operators to disseminate the information to employees so that they can implement proper food safety measures.

Source: *Pater* (2000)

2 Based on the case study, what measures can food-service organisations take to ensure that the quality and safety of food handling is 'fully up to par'?

Measures to ensure the quality and safety of food handling:

Feedback

Task 1

Typical activities for instilling an effective, quality-based health, safety and environmental culture could include the following:

- including health, safety and environment in the mission statement and business strategy
- developing Health and Safety Executive (HSE) quality systems based on ISO standards
- having a department for health, safety and the environment
- linking health, safety and the environment to team and individual performance
- developing joint consultation processes
- disseminating information on health, safety and the environment, for example, through a newsletter, via noticeboards or by e-mail
- empowering individuals to take responsibility for health, safety and the environment in their work areas
- carrying out health, safety and the environment promotional activities such as a health and safety improvement week
- increasing health, safety and environmental training.

You might consider extending this activity by using the above points to assess your own organisation. What improvements does your organisation need to make?

Task 2

From the case study, the measures food-service organisations can take to ensure that the quality and safety of food handling is fully up to standard include:

- using technology such as quick chillers and food temperature probes
- sanitising kitchen features such as equipment and utensils
- colour coding to separate different uses of utensils and equipment
- preventative and problem-based training
- educational seminars and safety kits.

◆ Recap

Assess how a quality approach can improve health, safety and environmental practices

◆ The same systematic approach that is taken to managing and improving quality can be applied to managing health, safety and the environment. This includes policy making, organising, planning and implementing, measuring performance, reviewing and auditing.

◆ Both the ISO 14000 series – the accepted international standard for environmental management – and the standards surrounding health and safety are built on the same principles as the quality management standards ISO 9000.

Identify ways of improving your health, safety and environmental culture

◆ As well as creating the systems for managing health, safety and the environment, an organisation and its managers need to promote and foster a culture that takes the issues seriously.

►► More @

To ensure you are meeting health and safety responsibilities in your own area, try the website for the **Health and Safety Executive** for information and resources, www.hse.gov.uk

References

Armstrong, A. (1990) *Management Processes and Functions*, CIPD

Bristol-Myers Squibb, 'Management Systems: EHS Management System', www.bms.com/static/ehs/manage/data/ehsman.html

Business Wire (2001a) 'Intermec Introduces Comprehensive Mobile Computing System for Logistics Industry', 9 May

Business Wire (2001b) 'VelQuest Announces Collaboration with AstraZeneca: Opening the Door to a Paperless Laboratory Environment', 6 March

Cauldron, S. *Just Exactly What Is Total Quality Management?* http://mars.acnet.wnec.edu/~achelte/tqm.htm

Crosby, P. B. (1979) *Quality is Free*, McGraw-Hill

Dale, B. and Cooper, C. (1992), *Total Quality and Human Resources: An executive guide*, Blackwell

Deming, W. E. (1986) *Out of Crisis*, MIT Center for Engineering Study

Donahue, A. (1999) 'E-Commerce Firms Grapple With Inventory Issues', *Los Angeles Business Journal*, Vol. 21, Iss. 44, November, 15

Irish Times (2000) 'Europe: Teamworking is Key to Company Success', May 1

European Foundation for Quality Management, *EFQM Excellence Model*, www.efqm.org

Feigenbaum, A. V. (1986) *Total Quality Control*, McGraw-Hill

Ford Motor Company, 'Our mission', www.ford.co.uk

Garvin, D. (1984) 'What Does "Product Quality" Really Mean', *Sloan Management Review*, Fall

Health and Safety Executive (1993) *Successful Health & Safety Management*, HSE Books

Health and Safety Executive, *Good Neighbour Scheme – A guide for employers*, www.hse.gov.uk/events/gnscheme.htm

Health and Safety Executive (2000) Press Release E026:00: HSE Publishes Report on MOX Fuel Data Falsification at BNFL, Sellafield, 18 February

Hill, T. (2000) *Operations Management*, Macmillan

Imai, M. (1986) *Kaizen: The Key to Japan's Competitive Success*, McGraw-Hill

Imai, M. (1997), Gemba *Kaizen: A Commonsense, Low-Cost Approach to Management*, McGraw-Hill

International Organization for Standardization, *ISO 8402*: 1994 (replaced by ISO 9000:2000), www.iso.ch

Juran Institute, www.juran.com

Laabs, J. J. (1998), 'Quality Drives Trident's Success', *Workforce*, February, Vol. 77, No. 2, 44–5

Manzaroli, T. (2001) 'DaimlerChrysler suffers quality woes: warranty costs surge as managers cut development times', *Financial Times* MarketWatch.com (Europe) Ltd, 8 May

Marshall, C. J., and Bentz, J. S. (1998) Abstracts: American Society of Cytopathology ', *Acta Cytologica: The Journal of Clinical Cytology and Cytopathology*, www.acta-cytol.com/Abs/ASC/ASC436.htm

Marx, K. (1859) *A Contribution to the Critique of the Political Economy*, Progress Publishers, transcribed for the Internet by zodiac@interlog.com

Mitchell, M. and Fairbanks, S. (2000) 'Kaizen is a CD hit', *Tooling & Production*, Adams/Huebcore Publishing Inc., December, Vol. 66, Iss. 9, 21

National Aeronautical and Space Administration, 'NASA's Services and Products and Customers Served', *NASA Customer Service Plan*, www.hq.nasa.gov

New Jersey Manufacturing Extension Program Inc. (NJMEP), 'APW Mclean is Going Lean', www.njmep.org

New Zealand Game Industry Board, 'DeerQA: Focusing on Customers' Needs and Perceptions', www.nzgib.org.nz/index.cfm

New Zealand Game Industry Board, 'DeerQA: Two Complementary Roles', www.nzgib.org.nz/index.cfm

Oakland, J. (2003) 3rd edition, *TWM: Text with Cases*, Butterworth-Heinmann

Packaging Magazine (2000) '"World first" for plastic', United Business Media International Ltd, 5 April

Pater, K. (2000) 'The Safety Zone', *Restaurants & Institutions*, Cahners Publishing Company, 15 June, Vol. 110, Iss. 16, 93

PC Week (2000) 'Tool predicts network capacity', Ziff-Davis Publishing Company, 10 January

Peters, T. and Austin, N. (1984) *A Passion for Excellence*, HarperCollins

Peters, T. and Waterman, R. (1982) *In Search of Excellence*, HarperCollins

Ridley, J. (1994) 4th edition, *Safety at Work*, Butterworth-Heinemann

Rodger, I. (2000) 'Outdoing the hackers' *BBC News Online: Business*, Friday, 24 March

Slack, N., Chambers, S. and Johnson, R. (2001) 3rd edition, *Operations Management*, FT Prentice Hall

TVS Suzuki Ltd, 'Quality', www.tvssuzuki.com/html/sotqc.htm

US Army – www.hqda.army.mil/leadingchange – for US Army's Strategic Management Initiative TAQ

Washington Cold Storage Inc., *'Mission Statement'*, www.washingtoncoldstorage.com/mission.html

Wild, T. (2002) *Best Practice in Inventory Management*, Elsevier Butterworth-Heinemann

Unisys/Management Today 2000 Service Excellence Awards (2000) 'Winner: Woburn Safari Park: Consumer services', Management Publications Ltd., September

Printed and bound by CPI Group (UK) Ltd, Croydon, CR0 4YY

22/10/2024

01777390-0001